ICNC **MONOGRAPH** SERIES

How Social Trust Shapes Civil Resistance

Lessons from Africa

Jacob S. Lewis

Contents

List of Key Terms and Their Definitions i

Introduction 1

    Activists, Organizations, and Campaigns 4

    Studying Trust 5

    Contributions 5

Chapter 1: A Theory of Social Trust and Civil Resistance 7

    How Does Trust Operate? 10

    Social Trust and Civil Resistance 12

    The Argument 14

        Social Trust and Willingness to Protest 14

        Social Trust and the Justification of Violent Action 16

    Expectations for This Study 18

Chapter 2: Trust and Participation in Nonviolent Protest 19

    Model and Data 19

    Descriptive Evidence 23

    Statistical Model 25

    Results 26

    Does Potential Mobilization Correlate with Actual Mobilization? 28

    Summary of Chapter 2 Findings 32

Chapter 3: Trust and Nonviolent Action 34

    Trust and Justification for Violent Action at the Individual Level 36

        Model and Data 37

        Results 37

Trust and Observed Nonviolent Discipline	**39**
Model and Data	**40**
Results	**46**
Summary of Chapter 3 Findings	**49**

Conclusion — **52**

    Relevant Findings for Activists — **52**

    Relevant Findings for Scholars — **54**

References — **56**

Statistical Appendix — **65**

    Overview — **65**

    Statistical Information from Chapter 2 — **65**

    Statistical Information from Chapter 3 — **68**

    Statistical Information for the Conclusion — **72**

    Do Survey Respondents Believe That They Are Speaking to a Government Agent? — **72**

Tables and Figures

TABLE 1. **Observations in Afrobarometer Rounds 3–5**	**20**
TABLE 2. **Results for Trust and Potential Mobilization Using the Full Sample**	**26**
TABLE 3. **Expected Relationships Between Trust and Justification of Violent Action**	**35**
TABLE 4. **Results for Trust and Justifications of Violent Action**	**38**
TABLE 5. **Afrobarometer Rounds and Years**	**42**
TABLE 6. **Prediction Results**	**52**
TABLE 7. **Descriptive Statistics for Trust Variables**	**65**
TABLE 8. **Linear Regression of Potential Mobilization with Full Sample**	**66**
TABLE 9. **Descriptive Statistics of Ingroup and Outgroup Trust Variables**	**68**

TABLE 10. Linear Regression on Justification of Violent Action	69
TABLE 11. Linear Regression on Proportion of Conflict That is Violent	71
TABLE 12. Union Membership and Trust in Diverse Populations	72
FIGURE 1. Proposed Explanations for How Trust Shapes Perceptions of Cost	16
FIGURE 2. Willingness to Attend a Protest	21
FIGURE 3. Different Measurements of Social Trust and Reported Potential Mobilization	24
FIGURE 4. Potential and Actual Mobilization	31
FIGURE 5. Justification of Violent Action	36
FIGURE 6. Social Trust and Justifications of Violent Action	39
FIGURE 7. Proportion of Antigovernment Contention That is Violent and Nonviolent	43
FIGURE 8. Generalized Trust and Predicted Antigovernment Nonviolent and Violent Actions	46
FIGURE 9. Trust in Diverse Groups and Predicted Nonviolent Contention	47
FIGURE 10. Comparison of Cross-Country Coefficients for Potential Mobilization	67
FIGURE 11. Comparison of Cross-Country Coefficients for Justification of Violent Action	70

List of Key Terms and Their Definitions

Generalized social trust refers to an individual's overall level of trust in other people, regardless of whether he or she personally knows them. In this monograph, generalized social trust is measured via a question in which individuals have to decide whether "most people can be trusted" or whether "you have to be very careful" when dealing with people.

Trust in co-nationals refers to a form of generalized social trust that extends to fellow citizens of one's country, regardless of whether he or she knows them. In this monograph, trust in co-nationals is measured via a question in which individuals rank how much they trust other citizens of their country from "not at all" to "a lot."

Trust in neighbors refers to a form of more particularized social trust that extends to one's neighbors. Like trust in co-nationals, this is measured from "not at all" to "a lot."

Trust in acquaintances refers to a form of more particularized social trust that extends to one's personal acquaintances, or "people you know." Like co-national trust, this is measured from "not at all" to "a lot."

Trust in diverse populations is defined as a form of generalized social trust that extends to individuals within a respondent's country that do not share the respondent's ethnic identity. Like co-national trust, this is measured from "not at all" to "a lot."

Correlation is a statistical term that designates a mathematical relationship between two measurements of social phenomena. Importantly, correlation does not imply a causal relationship.

Activist is used in this monograph to refer to individual participants—or potential participants—in civil resistance activities or organizations.

Organization (civil resistance organization) is used in this monograph to refer to established groups of civil resistance activists that pursue a common goal. They are characterized by the existence of some set of norms and leadership structure that govern how activists within the organization behave. For example, the African National Congress operated—at least for part of its existence—as a nonviolent civil resistance organization. More recently, the civil resistance campaign in Sudan in 2018 through 2019 was spearheaded in part by the Sudanese Professionals Association (SPA), which is an established organization within civil society.

Campaigns refer to the collective efforts, including nonviolent resistance actions—often coordinated—that are pursued by civil resistance organizations against state actors with a larger, often pro-democracy, goal. A recent example comes from Mali, where the 5 June Movement – Rally of Patriotic Forces (M5-RFP) served as an umbrella for multiple civil resistance organizations.

Protests are broadly defined as nonviolent demonstrations by citizens, activists, and civil resistance organizations targeting the government with particular claims or demands. Protest events are considered nonviolent if the actions of the protestors can reasonably be described as peaceful, even if the protest was violently repressed by state forces.

Potential mobilization refers to the stated willingness of an individual to join a nonviolent protest or demonstration.

Actual mobilization refers to whether an individual actually participated in a nonviolent protest or demonstration.

Nonviolent discipline refers to the capacity of participants in protests to refuse to use violent actions and tactics, even when faced with government repression.

Introduction

The end of the Cold War, propelled by mass mobilizations in Eastern and Central European societies, brought about renewed scholarly and policy interest in the role that "people power" movements could play in toppling dictatorships and ushering in democracies throughout the world. These works focused on the important role that nonviolent civil resistance has played in driving successful political transitions (Schock 1999, 2005). Civil resistance refers to the "sustained use of methods of nonviolent action by civilians engaged in asymmetric conflicts with opponents not averse to using violence to defend their interests" (Schock 2013).[1] An emerging body of quantitative study on civil resistance has emphasized the effectiveness of civil resistance as a strategy for opposing repressive and authoritarian regimes. Chenoweth and Stephan's (2011) work detailed that nonviolent civil resistance is often more successful than violent insurrections. Despite setbacks in post–Arab Spring democratization efforts, Pinckney (2018) showed that when nonviolent civil resistance is paired with a durable network of activists and civil society, post-transition democracies are more likely to consolidate and thrive.

The study of civil resistance has become increasingly important as democratic norms have begun to weaken around the world and authoritarian leaders have directly challenged the global liberal democratic order. All around the world, civil resistance movements are rising to meet the challenges of an increasingly organized and coordinated authoritarian assault on civil liberties and democratic government. In Hong Kong throughout 2019 and 2020, citizens took to the streets to protest the growing influence of Beijing in curtailing freedoms and accountability, and specifically the introduction of an extradition law that would undercut Hong Kong's democratic autonomy (Ramzy and Ives 2020). In the United States, a multiracial coalition of activists has demanded an end to systemic racism and police brutality (Buchanan, Bui, and Patel 2020). And in Zimbabwe, activists are peacefully demanding an end to corruption and violence as the government has sought to consolidate its control and stifle freedom (Africa Research Bulletin 2020b). Indeed, Africa has witnessed numerous civil resistance movements over the past decade that have helped challenge and even topple or defeat corrupt regimes, including in Algeria, South Africa, Mali, and Sudan.

The growing readiness of people to resort to civil resistance across the globe commands a concurrent expansion in scholarship and analysis. Research has focused largely on how campaigns operate, succeed, or fail. Work on these micro-dynamics has examined

---

1 Central to civil resistance is the maintenance of nonviolent discipline. This may be principled and moralistic, as proposed by Gregg (2018) or strategic, as proposed by Sharp (1973).

within-movement fractures (Bramsen 2018), decision-making (Dudouet 2015), and maintaining nonviolent discipline (Bramsen 2019; Pinckney 2016). One important area of scholarship in conflict studies and democracy that has been understudied in the context of civil resistance is that of trust. A large body of research has focused on how trust shapes political behaviors (Caillier 2010), community development and democracy (Putnam 2001; Sønderskov 2011a; Sønderskov and Dinesen 2016), and collective action (Nilson and Nilson 1980; Sønderskov 2009; van Stekelenburg and Klandermans 2018). Despite this literature, scholars and activists have not explored trust in-depth with regard to important questions in civil resistance. As a result, there are many important areas of inquiry in which the application of micro-level analysis may be fruitful. For example, recent work by Chenoweth and Ulfelder (2017) tests whether major theories in conflict studies and contentious politics help explain the onset of mass civil resistance movements. They find that while some theories outperform others, none of the extant theories tested thoroughly explain the onset of such movements. Similarly, scholars and activists know very little beyond Pinckney's (2016) recent findings of why some campaigns are able to maintain nonviolent discipline while others are not.

This monograph represents an attempt to fold the study of political psychology into mainstream civil resistance scholarship. In doing so, it focuses primarily on the role that different forms of social trust might play in shaping civil resistance in Africa. Research on civil resistance will benefit greatly from increased interest in the notion of social trust. At the level of the individual activist, studying trust can tell activists and scholars alike about the micro-level dynamics that shape when individuals decide to engage, how they decide to engage, and more. And studies of trust at the group level could reveal important information about the development of cultures of trust that moderate group behavior and shape possibilities for collaboration with other organizations in the midst of a country-wide campaign.

This study fills in an important gap in the existing research by focusing on trust as a key element that shapes the development—and success—of civil resistance campaigns. While using the term trust, this study adopts a definition that incorporates rationalist and moralist definitions. Rationalist definitions define trust as the belief by an individual that another individual will honor his or her obligations or promises. Moralist definitions of trust instead focus on how individuals evaluate the moral character of others and deem them to be trustworthy. The rationalist and moralist views of trust complement one another, providing both "thin" transactional and "thick" moral reasoning to explain how high levels of trust may shape participation in civil resistance, as well as why it may be important in shaping nonviolent discipline. Within this framework, one conceives of a "moral community," which can be narrow (e.g., comprising only one's family, friends, or ethnic groups) or broad (e.g., comprising large swaths of a community). For example, a rationalist activist with high trust may strategically shape her behavior around the assumption that her civil resistance organization will remain strategically faithful to their pre-determined pact for nonviolent action. As such, she maintains nonviolent discipline, even in the face of potential repression. A moralist activist with high trust may interpret the identical situation differently, but come to the conclusion that members of his moral community share a commitment to nonviolent action and would not violate that norm.

This study centers its attention on examining how levels of trust held by individuals across Africa might affect their behavior in mass movements and civil resistance campaigns. In particular, it focuses on how trust might shape the potential for Africans to engage in nonviolent protests and demonstrations, as well as their attitudes toward nonviolent discipline. Why should activists, civil society organizations, and policymakers care about trust when considering civil resistance? Civil resistance movements are, by their nature, collective and social activities that often take place in environments of low trust and high risk. In some cases, civil resistance movements—or at least some of its key members—are forced to remain clandestine in order to protect against possible government repression and detention. In other cases, such movements operate openly and under the scrutiny of the public eye. In both of these cases, civil resistance movements in which members trust one another and also trust the group leaders are most likely to thrive. There are several reasons that trust likely matters:

Trust may alter the perceived costs of participation. Chenoweth and Stephan's (2011) argument hinges largely on the role that nonviolent civil resistance plays in reducing the perceived costs of participating in civil resistance campaigns in comparison to armed resistance campaigns. Nonviolent tactics often entail lower physical demands on participants, are more easily communicated and coordinated, and impose fewer moral concerns. Yet, governments do not always respond to nonviolent action accordingly. In the early 1990s, the Nigerian government responded to the nonviolent Movement for the Survival of the Ogoni People's protests against environmental destruction and corruption with violent reprisals and, in the end, the murder of nine activists, including Ken Saro-Wiwa (Onuoha 2012; Osha 2006). These are high prices to pay, and yet Southern Nigerians have continued to organize against the government in the thirty years since. One potential explanation for this continued resistance is that high levels of social trust have helped develop what Uslaner (2002) calls *moral communities*, in which potential activists not only trust the moral character of civil resistance organizers but feel an acute sense of missing out by not joining in (Aytac and Stoke 2019). When trust is high in such moral communities, potential activists may perceive the costs of participation to be lower. Trust may alleviate fears of being "the only one to show up for a protest" or it might strengthen social solidarities. Fortunately, a large body of trust research helps to explain these dynamics.

Trust may be essential to remaining nonviolent in the face of violent repression. Nonviolent discipline[2] requires participants in social movement and activist groups to maintain trust along several lines. Individuals that are considering mobilizing into an activist group are often drawn in through networks of *individual* or *peer trust* (McAdam 1986). Generalized social trust[3] (Uslaner 2002, 2008) likely shapes what types of groups a non-mobilized individual is willing to participate in. General levels of peer trust within a social network may shape successful efforts to mobilize that individual.[4] High levels of social trust likely make it easier for potential activists to feel confident that a civil resistance organization or campaign will honor its commitment to nonviolent discipline. High levels of social trust may also result in a larger conception of a moral community,[5] reducing the incentive to use violent tactics to make political demands. High-trusting groups may be better able to sanction potential defectors and provocateurs because their members are familiar with one another and thus do not need to expend the resources to monitor each member constantly. Dense trust networks likely make it easier to identify behaviors that do not conform with norms of nonviolent action. Different groups will develop different *cultures of trust* that shape whether activists within the group can remain nonviolent,[6] particularly as tensions begin to run high and repression is used. Government repression can put enormous strain on civil resistance organizations and campaigns, and civil resistance organizations populated by high-trusting activists may be better able to negotiate differences of opinion while remaining committed to nonviolent action.

Activists, Organizations, and Campaigns

This monograph refers regularly to three different types of actors engaged in civil resistance. First, the monograph refers to *activists*, by which is meant individual members of civil resistance organizations. The majority of the monograph looks at the beliefs and trust sentiments of individual activists, which is a departure from most work on civil resistance that would usually consider a collective or a movement. Second, the monograph refers to *organizations*

---

2   For more on nonviolent discipline, see Pinckney's *Making or Breaking Nonviolent Discipline* (2016).

3   See the list of key definitions for more on generalized social trust and how it relates to other measures of trust.

4   A crucial component of social capital (Putnam 2001).

5   As described in the following chapter, a moral community refers to a group within society that an individual feels possesses moral views or beliefs that makes them trustworthy. No direct trusting relationship is required; for example, someone may believe that members of a religious congregation or a labor union are inherently trustworthy because of the morals that they hold. That same individual need not have any direct interaction with them or any reason to place trust in them apart from those morals.

6   See Schock (2005) for more detail on how nonviolent civil resistance may be deployed pragmatically rather than as a moral principle, as put forth by Gregg (2018). Sharp (2013) details many nonviolent 'weapons' that can be deployed by activists.

as specific groups that engage in civil resistance against a government. Organizations, such as South Africa's African National Congress (ANC), generally have formalized names, leadership structures, and even branding. Finally, by *campaigns,* the monograph refers to the collective efforts of civil resistance organizations to bring about some major political or social change. In South Africa, the United Democratic Front (UDF) served as an umbrella campaign made up of multiple organizations seeking the end of apartheid.

Studying Trust

Studying the role of trust in civil resistance presents a number of challenges. First, because trust is a psychological factor, it is inherently difficult to measure. At the level of individual activists, survey data can be used to measure the correlation between reported levels of trust. This approach provides relatively direct access to self-reported levels of trust, but it does not provide insight into how trust actually shapes behavior. This monograph makes two specific efforts to correct for this. Studying trust at the level of civil resistance organizations and campaigns is substantially more difficult. Gathering evidence about levels of trust by using secondary and tertiary sources injects major concerns in data quality. While scattered interviews with activists may provide insight into the social dynamics within a civil resistance organization or even a campaign, this evidence is rare and retrospective. Additionally, examining case studies and ascribing organizational dynamics and behaviors to trust introduces a substantial risk of confirmation bias. In order to maximize confidence in the measurement of trust, this monograph takes the decision to rely on individual-level reports of trust. While this does limit the ability of the monograph to make generalizations about campaigns, it provides greater internal validity with regard to the study of trust, willingness to participate in nonviolent protests, and whether individuals believe that violent action is justified.

Contributions

This monograph makes a number of contributions that should be helpful to activists and scholars alike. First, this monograph focuses on civil resistance in Africa, drawing data and several small cases from the continent. This contributes to a growing movement to extend our knowledge of civil resistance beyond Europe and North America (Chabot and Vinthagen 2015), focusing on Africa, a vast continent with a rich tradition and culture of nonviolent resistance despite violence and wars that tend to dominate the airwaves of the mainstream media about Africa. The anti-apartheid civil resistance campaign is perhaps Africa's most well-known case, but many other important civil resistance campaigns helped shape Africa's independence movements and the pro-democracy campaigns that emerged following the end of the Cold War. Since 2010, Africa has experienced a third wave of protest movements calling for an end to corruption, improvement in governance, and true economic growth. For activists operating in the developing world, this research acknowledges that many of the conditions faced in the Global South differ quite greatly from those in North America and Europe.

Second, this monograph examines individual-level psychological factors that may shape the onset and trajectory of civil resistance campaigns. It analyzes the relationship between social trust and two factors that are central to civil resistance. It looks at how trust shapes the willingness of individuals to engage in nonviolent protests and demonstrations. It then looks at how trust influences reported justifications for the use of violent political actions in general. In doing so, this monograph complements a body of work that has examined how social ties shape civil resistance. Trust and social ties are likely highly related, but they are theoretically and functionally distinct, and thus trust merits independent attention. The monograph also provides a multi-level analysis. It begins by examining the relationship at the individual level. It then uses observed data on protest behavior and conflict to examine: (a) whether expressed willingness to participate in nonviolent protests correlates with actual, observed levels of protest behavior across Africa, and (b) whether regions in which citizens express high levels of social trust experience higher proportions of nonviolent conflict than regions in which citizens express low levels of social trust.

The findings of this monograph support the argument that social trust is beneficial for civil resistance in two ways. First, high levels of social trust correspond with increased reported willingness to participate in nonviolent protests. Civil resistance organizations have often emerged from existing social networks, in which trust is developed between members. Second, high levels of social trust correspond with an increased commitment to nonviolent action. This finding is consistent when analyzed at the individual level and when analyzed using a dataset of observed protests across Africa. The monograph finds evidence that individuals with high levels of trust in diverse populations (i.e., individuals who do not share their ethnicity) are less likely to express that violent action can be justified. Bramsen (2018) does find that the mobilization of diverse groups within society increase the likelihood of success, and the findings of this monograph suggest that if activists can mobilize individuals who demonstrate high levels of trust in diverse populations, they may be able to improve nonviolent discipline. This may entail reframing civil resistance communications and messaging to highlight commonly shared grievances or to promote messages of unity.

Chapter 1: A Theory of Social Trust and Civil Resistance

Trust serves as a core connective tissue that keeps societies together. Past scholarship in political science has focused on trust relationships at two different levels. First, scholars considered how the amount of trust that a population has in its government shapes interpersonal trust. Levi (1998) provides an important overview of the role that a trustworthy government can play in reducing transaction costs that would otherwise require citizens to be wary not only of the government but of one another.[7] By this, the idea is that trustworthy governments can enforce contracts made between private citizens. Trustworthy governments not only facilitate the possibility of positive exchanges between any given citizen and the government but also reassure citizens that others are following the rules and not shirking their social obligations. For example, trustworthy governments can serve as the backend of commitments made by citizens to one another, such as when they enforce legal agreements and financial transactions.

Of course, many governments are untrustworthy. Throughout Africa—as in much of the developing world—governments routinely serve their own interests rather than those of their constituents. For example, African "strongman" leaders such as Robert Mugabe of Zimbabwe, Paul Biya of Cameroon, and Jacob Zuma of South Africa often treated state coffers as means for personal enrichment rather than for state development (Godwin 2011; Madonsela 2016; O'Donnell and Gramer 2018). Corruption and human rights abuses run rampant, and citizens begin to lose trust not only in their governments but often with one another (Levi 1998). This dismantling of trust produces contradictory outcomes. As governments become less capable or willing to serve as the guarantor of interpersonal relations, generalized social trust between strangers becomes more difficult and rare. At the same time, communities are forced to develop particularized trust networks built around specific communities in order to meet their needs.

Thus, trust (or lack thereof) in government bleeds into society more generally. When societies have high levels of trust, they build social capital (Putnam 2001) and improve

---

[7] Levi draws from Douglass North's (1984, 1991) seminal work on how institutions serve to reduce transaction costs between strangers, thereby allowing modern societies to function. In short, if Citizen A can trust that a government agency will faithfully enforce a transaction with Citizen B, then Citizens A and B do not need to spend significant effort vetting one another. When trust that the government can or will enforce private interactions declines, Citizens A and B become reluctant to interact with one another. This is often applied to private financial transactions, but can also be applied to the enforcement of laws. If Citizens A and B have a car accident and neither law enforcement nor the judiciary can be trusted to faithfully mediate the dispute (perhaps demanding bribes to rule in favor of one or another), both will find themselves unable to interact trustingly within society.

associational life (Sønderskov 2011a).[8] As such, high-trust networks that often characterize associational life can be extremely important. Such associations within civil society often support the founding of, or even serve as, civil resistance organizations that cooperate within a larger civil resistance campaign. In the African context, such associational life has proven to be of fundamental importance in challenging unjust governments. Strong civil society—including religious congregations and labor unions—often served as vanguards to the transition to multiparty democratic rule across the post-colonial states in the 1990s (Larmer 2009; Thompson 2014). These elements of society were often too powerful even for authoritarian one-party states to shutter.

This is particularly true in South Africa, where trade unions often served as the only legalized mechanism through which anti-apartheid black consciousness could prosper and persist. These trade unions struck early victories against the apartheid state in the mid-1980s and helped foster the skills and mobilization necessary to challenge the regime a decade later.[9] These unions remain influential today in South Africa, and the emergence of new unions has begun to challenge the ANC-dominated[10] government, particularly in the shadow of the 2012 massacre at Marikana.[11] The success of different elements of African civil society in challenging unjust governments would not have been possible without linkages of trust that fostered cooperation in rough and dangerous circumstances. Given that civil resistance movements not only focus on improving society by challenging unjust rule but also draw directly from society in order to do so, issues of trust should be at the forefront of civil resistance scholarship.[12]

The central role of such associational life suggests that trust serves an important role in facilitating the development, growth, and cohesion of civil resistance organizations and campaigns. While trust has been identified as important for cooperation in both lab and field

---

8   Associational life refers to voluntary collective organizations, ranging from bowling leagues to religious congregations to politically oriented civics groups.

9   This is detailed excellently in Leonard Thompson's (2014) *A History of South Africa*, beginning on page 224.

10   The African National Congress is the liberation party that won power in South Africa's first open elections in 1994 and has continued to dominate—albeit diminishingly—the political landscape in the country ever since. The ANC has become increasingly corrupt and inefficient. See Booysen (2015), Runciman (2016), and Alexander (2010) for more information on the manner in which South Africans have engaged in both violent and nonviolent civil resistance against the ANC.

11   In which 34 unarmed and partially armed miners were shot and killed (and numerous others wounded) by South African police following a wage dispute. Marikana shocked South Africans and galvanized anti-government activism in its wake. The authoritative account of the massacre can be found in Greg Marinovich's (2016) thorough and haunting *Murder at Small Koppie*. For information on the impact of Marikana on trade union activism, consider Luke Sinwell and Siphiwe Mbatha's (2016) *The Spirit of Marikana*.

12   Of course, trust is not exclusively the providence of pro-social, pro-democracy actors. Trust plays an important role in the cohesion of all types of groups—from civil resistance organizations to terrorist organizations.

settings (Axelrod 2006; Habyarimana et al. 2009), and also in shaping policies (Cook, Hardin, and Levi 2005; Lubell 2007), theories of trust do not feature prominently in works on civil resistance. Yet, many questions about the role that trust plays in civil resistance movements speak to central issues that are important to both activists and scholars alike. For example, how do different types of trust shape individual preferences over mobilization or the use of violent or nonviolent tactics? There is reason to believe that such relationships exist. Individual-level factors and preferences, such as social networks, matter in shaping mobilization, as has been widely demonstrated (Corrigall-Brown 2011; Gould 1991, 1993, 1995; Viterna 2006; Wickham-Crowley 1992). For civil resistance activists and scholars, better understanding these relationships can improve efforts to attract new members, improve the selection of members, and provide new avenues for research.

This monograph examines these questions in the context of civil resistance campaigns waged in Africa, stretching from the early 20th century through the most recent third wave of resistance. Africa has experienced three major waves of protest and civil resistance. The first wave took place during the end of the colonial period, as civil resistance movements rose across Africa in order to challenge colonialism and demand independence. While some liberation movements embraced violent tactics, many opted for nonviolent civil resistance, such as the Zambian anti-colonial movement (Momba and Gadsden 2013) and the Ghanaian independence movement (Presbey 2013).

Trade unions struck early victories against the apartheid state in the mid-1980s and helped foster the skills and mobilization necessary to challenge the regime a decade later.

The second wave emerged as the Cold War came to a close (Ihonvbere 1996; Mueller 2018) and Africans across the continent demanded true democratic transition. These demands focused on breaking the de facto authoritarian one-party systems and establishing a multiparty democratic rule in their place (Bratton and van de Walle 1997). Africa's third wave began to develop in 2010 alongside the Arab Spring (Branch and Mampilly 2015) and has been characterized by renewed demands for truly democratic reforms, improved economic conditions, and an end to corruption. During Africa's third wave, several notable civil resistance movements were instrumental in removing leaders from power. In South Africa, anger over corruption led to sustained civil resistance campaigns against then-president Jacob Zuma and his blatant corruption, which led the ruling ANC to replace him with Cyril Ramaphosa. From late 2018 to mid-2019, an admirable civil resistance campaign took root in Sudan against Omar al-Bashir, resulting in his removal from power by the military. In Algeria in 2019, following the declaration of President Abdelaziz Bouteflika's intention to run for a fifth term in office, a broad campaign engaged in sustained protests and filled the streets of Algiers. Bouteflika was deposed by the military as a result of these nonviolent protests (Hussein 2019). And in 2020, the June 5 Movement in Mali organized primarily (though not entirely) nonviolent and sustained protests against President Ibrahim Boubacar Keïta, resulting in the military arresting and deposing him (Africa Research Bulletin 2020a).

This chapter presents an overview of past scholarship that has examined the ways in which trust shapes societies and collective actions such as participation in protests. This review provides a framework to better understand how and why trust might be an important topic of study for activists and scholars interested in civil resistance. Two competing approaches to understanding trust (rational trust versus moral trust) are presented and examples of how these different approaches would inform any study of trust and civil resistance are provided. After reviewing the literature, the monograph then proposes two arguments about how trust might matter for civil resistance. First, an argument is presented that higher levels of social trust likely correspond to the increased willingness of individuals to engage in nonviolent protests and demonstrations. Second, an argument is presented that higher levels of social trust are likely to improve nonviolent discipline, which is a central feature of civil resistance.

How Does Trust Operate?

A large body of scholarship has focused on the determinants and effects of generalized social trust in society. One common way to think about trust is as a rational expectation about the behavior of someone else. Rationalist approaches to trust generally operate on a transactional basis, in which "A trusts B to do X" (Levi 1998, 78). This is a rather thin approach to understanding trust.[13] Using this approach, trustworthiness is wrapped up in the idea that two parties—the truster and the trustee—will benefit by working together.[14] The core motivation of rational trust is personal benefit or gain. In other words, we trust those whom we believe are motivated to remain trustworthy in part for personal gain. For the civil resistance activist, this rational trust operates as follows: when deciding whether to mobilize and attend a demonstration, a member of a civil resistance group trusts that other members of the group will, indeed, show up for the demonstration. If the other members do show up, the activist's trust has been fulfilled and the shared objective (the demonstration) succeeds. If they do not, that activist will be alone, holding signs by herself in the square, and thus the expected mass demonstration is unsuccessful.

For activists and members of civil resistance organizations, rational trust may not provide a meaningful or satisfactory definition of trust or the role that it plays in facilitating the onset

---

13   Scholars often refer to rational trust as "encapsulated trust."

14   This approach gained great support during the surge of rational choice theorization in the social sciences. Giants such as Russell Hardin, Margaret Levi, Karen Cook, and Elinor Ostrom detailed rationalist arguments in a collection of books that were published as the *Russell Sage Foundation Series on Trust*.

and growth of organizations and campaigns. Rational trust can feel thin and fragile, and while it may adequately describe interactions between individuals in isolated or one-off circumstances, it is less useful in explaining how trust operates at the organizational or campaign level. This chapter presents two additional approaches that shed light on how civil resistance organizations and campaigns operate. First, it discusses how trust networks—dense and often secretive groups that operate with purpose—shapes how civil resistance organizations start and operate in difficult and dangerous environments. Second, it discusses the idea of moral trust, which helps explain how large campaigns, full of disparate organizations and activists, retain trust even when campaigns experience setbacks.

When activists in civil resistance organizations pursue moral ends such as democratic transitions, they place trust in the idea that their fellow activists are participating for reasons beyond personal gain.

For civil resistance activists—particularly those in repressive or corrupt countries—relationships of trust may be built into *trust networks*, as detailed by Charles Tilly (2005). Trust networks are characterized by four primary criteria that can aptly describe civil resistance movements. First, networks are comprised of individuals with either direct connections to one another or indirect connections (via an intermediary). Second, each member of the network demonstrates a credible commitment to the overall goals or interests of the trust network. In a civil resistance organization, these first two criteria describe the organizational membership, structure, and cohesive bonds that link them together. Third, members of trust networks are responsible for working together over time in what Tilly describes as long-term enterprises. Thus, a single, one-off demonstration cannot be part of a network. Finally—and perhaps most importantly for activists at risk of repression or detention—the close ties of membership also generate potential concerns of exposure to a repressive government. Put simpler, trust networks based on the knowledge and acquaintanceship of its members are risky—they carry with them the strength of collective effort, including mutual trust, built over time, but also risk network-wide exposure if any individual member is captured. As a result, trust plays a critical role in selecting and maintaining membership.

An additional alternative to rational trust is moral trust. This largely refers to the expectation that we fulfill trust obligations for moral reasons in addition to rational or self-interested reasons. Uslaner (2002) speaks of moral communities that facilitate trust in others. The more we trust others, the larger our moral community becomes. Unlike the thin rational trust just discussed, moral trust is quite resilient, in part because individuals apply their trust beliefs across a community rather than to specific individuals. When activists in civil resistance organizations pursue moral ends such as democratic transitions, they place trust in the idea that their fellow activists are participating for reasons beyond personal gain. As such, moral trust is not founded on interpersonal transactions in the way that rational trust is and may explain the retention of trust relationships even when one member fails to fulfill (or, indeed, violates) the trust placed in them. Civil resistance organizations and campaigns likely operate as moral communities, with trust placed in the moral goals and aims of the campaign rather than the actions of individual activists or organizations. This form of trust makes it easier for campaigns to persist in the face of difficult situations; when a campaign temporarily falters or fails, members of the campaign remain trusting over the moral character of the campaign goal and are willing to remain engaged and committed.

Social Trust and Civil Resistance

There are, of course, many trust relationships in our daily lives. We may place very different levels of trust in society, our friends, family, and religious and ethnic groups. For the sake of this monograph, when the monograph discusses trust, it is discussing what scholars call generalized social trust. *Generalized social trust* (social trust hereafter) describes the trust relationship between an individual and his or her expectations of the trustworthiness of others throughout society. Thus, an individual with high levels of social trust tends to believe the best of others, irrespective of who they are. Social trust can be evaluated with questions like, "in general, are most people trustworthy?" For those who respond in the affirmative, the implication is that most people are part of the respondent's moral community.

While research on civil resistance has not directly addressed the role of social trust, there is existing research in political science that provides a foundation upon which to base expectations. For example, social trust has been shown to increase cooperation (Sønderskov 2009, 2011b) and reduce preferences for violent radicalism (Glaeser 2016). Other research finds that trust corresponds with a number of contentious actions, including signing a petition, engaging in lawful demonstrations, engaging in unofficial strikes, and even occupying a building (Benson and Rochon 2004). Benson and Rochon argue that interpersonal trust might help solve the assurance puzzle embedded within protest,[15] namely that the expected utility of one's own participation is in part contingent on how many other participants show up. Because larger groups generally signal broader public support and greater overall resolve, it would be disadvantageous—and possibly damaging to the cause—to be the only activist to show up for a protest. They argue that high-trusting individuals are better able to predict the behavior of others, thus increasing their levels of assurance that other activists will, indeed, show up to protest.

---

15   For more information, see Chong's (1991) work on the civil rights movement.

Relatedly, scholarship in the fields of civil resistance and contentious politics has focused heavily on social networks and social linkages. Extensive work in sociology has emphasized the role of social networks in mobilizing bystanders into social movements (Gould 1991, 1993; Snow, Zurcher Jr., and Ekland-Olson 1980).[16] Marwell, Oliver, and Prahl (1988) demonstrate that the structural elements, including the density, centralization, and heterogeneity of social ties, shape prospects for collective action.[17]

Recent work by Thurber (2019) uses evidence from Nepal to argue that different types of social linkages shape whether resistance organizations can strategically rely on nonviolent actions. Whereas "insular" movements—those without broad connections to society or the regime—can easily be repressed, "integrated" movements cannot. Thurber argues that this affects whether such movements employ nonviolent civil resistance strategies or instead adopt armed violent actions. In the coming chapters, this monograph speaks to these findings by demonstrating that individuals with high levels of trust in diverse populations (suggesting openness to integrated movements) are significantly less likely to state that violent actions can be justified than individuals with low levels of trust in diverse populations.[18]

On the other hand, Lee and Glasure (2007) find that the linkage between associational membership (often thought to correlate with high social trust) and protest is weak and highly conditional. More recently, Glaeser (2016) found that the effect of social trust on protest is conditional. Glaeser observed that at the individual level, social trust is positively and statistically significantly correlated with intention to protest; however, when aggregated to the administrative district level, this relationship inverts. These findings provide a reason for caution and highlight the need for additional study, including the analysis conducted later in this monograph. Crepaz, Jazayeri, and Polk (2017) find that different types of trust help to shape political participation. High levels of ingroup trust positively correspond with voting behavior, while high levels of outgroup trust (referred to in this monograph as trust in diverse populations) correspond positively with "unconventional forms of political participation" such as protests.

In addition to clarifying some of these empirical puzzles, it is important to note that the study of trust, while related to social linkages and networks, is theoretically and empirically distinct and thus merits specific attention. One generally assumes that trust is a foundational

---

16 Of course, not all work on networks and mobilization focus on nonviolent civil resistance organizations and movements. In her seminal work on the 1994 Rwandan genocide, Fujii (2008) shows that social linkages can mobilize participation in ethnic cleansing. Fujii also demonstrates that cross-ethnic linkages often led genocidaires to warn potential victims whom they knew or were friendly with. This generates a strange tension, in which social linkages act simultaneously upon an agent to push them toward participating in genocide and simultaneously subverting genocide.

17 These authors do not address Granovetter's (1973) distinction between strong and weak ties. Granovetter's work on the strength of ties does suggest trust as a central component of strong ties.

18 See Chapter 3 for more on this.

element of most social linkages and networks, but this is not necessarily true. Whereas traditional theories of social trust assume that associations are likely comprised of "high-trusters," there are circumstances in which these assumptions may not hold. Labor unions are associational, but are formed via entry into a trade rather than via channels of shared interests. Alternatively, activists may actively distrust one another, but this distrust may be trumped by a greater distrust for the government, leading to a temporary alliance that dissolves at a later date. The focus on trust in this monograph thus merits attention distinct from existing attention paid to social networks and linkages.

The Argument

On the whole, however, scholarship suggests a positive relationship between social trust and participation in nonviolent protests, demonstrations, and other nonviolent actions. For activists and scholars of civil resistance, these findings provide a reason to believe that high levels of social trust benefit civil resistance at multiple levels. The monograph argues that social trust should be particularly important in shaping two elements of civil resistance. First, it argues that social trust is likely to increase the willingness of potential activists to participate in nonviolent protests and demonstrations. Second, it argues that social trust is likely to increase nonviolent discipline by reducing the willingness of individuals to justify violent actions. These arguments are presented in more detail below.

Social Trust and Willingness to Protest

It is expected that individuals with high levels of social trust would report a higher willingness to participate in protests and demonstrations. For the sake of this argumentation, the monograph will refer to the willingness to participate as *potential mobilization*. It is argued that from the perspective of civil resistance, social trust seems likely to increase the potential mobilization of African citizens. This is because social trust seems likely to generate a sense of solidarity with strangers that may either reduce the perceived costs of mobilization or may inoculate potential activists to those costs. Participating in civil resistance organizations and campaigns can be costly in numerous ways, and these costs may reduce potential mobilization by encouraging free-riding (Lichbach 1995; Olson 1965).[19] Activists also need to dedicate time and resources to organizing and engaging in civil resistance activities such as protests or demonstrations. And those activities can carry costs as well, including the risk of experiencing government repression.

---

19   In the study of collective action, free-riding describes the behavior of members of an organization or collective who do not contribute but still reap the benefits of being part of the organization.

There are several potential ways in which social trust may serve to solve the problem of high costs. First, social trust, conceived through the moral trust framework, may alter perceptions of those costs. High-trusting individuals may observe civil resistance groups engaging in protest and trust that their interests are the same as those of other protesters. That observer may assume that because their interests are in line, and thus they belong to the same moral community, the potential of somehow being betrayed by the group or put at risk by the group is low, and would therefore feel comfortable mobilizing. Chenoweth and Stephan (2011) argue that the nonviolent character of civil resistance can reduce the perceived costs of participation in anti-government activities such as protests, speeches, and noncooperation. Social trust may operate similarly, reducing the perceived costs of participating in civil resistance. High trusting groups may be able to operate under duress because trust itself serves to reduce both the incentives to violate group norms and the need to observe individual member behavior (Ensminger 2001). In this sense, trust plays the role of reducing within-group costs (time, resources) needed to monitor and enforce desired behavior (North 1984), whereas citizens who lack trust are unlikely to join a civil resistance organization or participate in a campaign without an established, formal leadership structure through which group norms and rules are enforced (Cook, Hardin, and Levi 2005).

There is a second, alternative way in which social trust may increase potential mobilization. Rather than altering the perceived costs of mobilization, social trust may serve to increase the price that any individual is willing to pay when engaging in civil resistance activities such as protests or demonstrations. In situations where one's moral community is being repressed by the police or a coercive government agency, citizens may decide that rather than simply worrying about the personal costs to them, they care more about standing up in solidarity with their fellow activists.[20] In fact, it might be that assaults on one's moral community increase what Aytac and Stokes (2019) call the "costs of abstention." These costs of abstention refer to the sense of missing out and the moral discomfort produced by not participating in a demonstration, protest, or other activity linked with civil resistance. McAdam's (1986) seminal work on the recruitment of participants into high-cost activism highlights the importance of "microstructures" such as organizational affiliation and personal connections in motivating participation in the Freedom Summer of 1964. For activists dedicated to civil resistance against a repressive regime or in favor of democratic transition, the answer to the question, "Why did you pay the costs of demonstrating against the government?" might very well be, "I couldn't afford not to."

Prediction 1: High levels of social trust correspond with an increased willingness to engage in nonviolent protests and demonstrations.

---

20 Scholars of contentious politics and civil resistance refer to this as "backlash" and "backfire," respectively (Daxecker and Hess 2013; Martin 2015).

Figure 1. Proposed Explanations for How Trust Shapes Perceptions of Cost displays the two proposed mechanisms suggested thus far. The perceived costs of participation (e.g., mobilizing, opportunity costs, potentially experiencing repression) are denoted in the blue continuous line while the willingness to pay those costs are denoted in the red dotted line. On the left, as trust increases (on the x-axis), the perceptions of the cost of participating in nonviolent protest diminish to the point of crossing the threshold of the willingness of an individual to pay those costs to participate. On the right, as trust increases, the willingness to pay the costs of participation increases until it surpasses the perceived costs of participation in nonviolent protest.

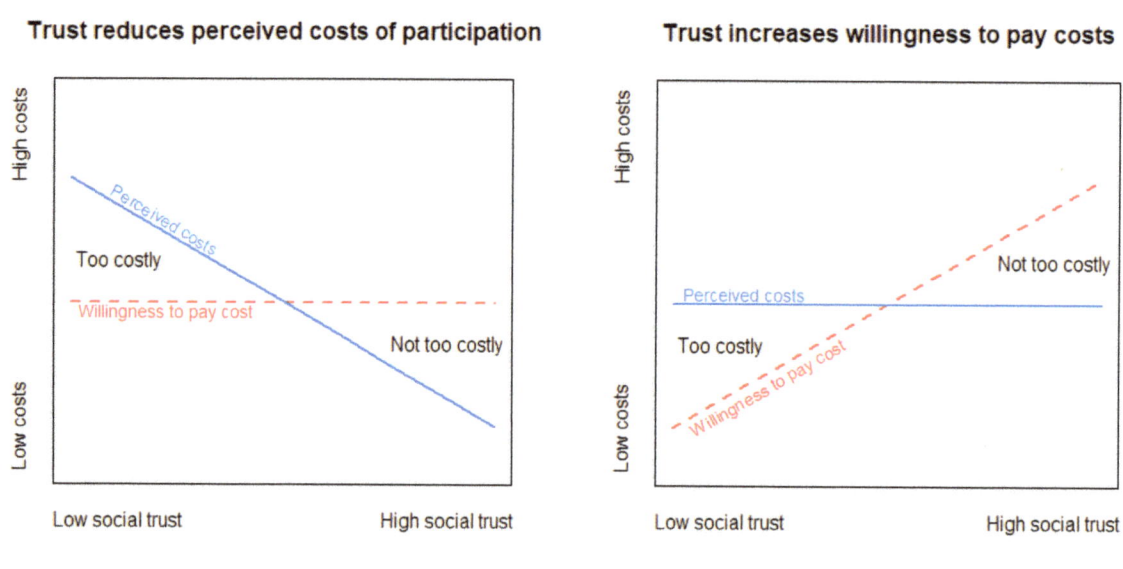

FIGURE 1. Proposed Explanations for How Trust Shapes Perceptions of Cost

Social Trust and the Justification of Violent Action

We now turn to a second argument about the role that social trust may play in shaping nonviolent discipline during civil resistance. One of the core tenets of civil resistance is the maintenance of nonviolent discipline by those who join and participate in campaigns and their actions. In short, civil resistance organizations eschew the use of violence in favor of a large portfolio of nonviolent actions, including peaceful demonstrations, strikes, sit-ins, and boycotts. Why would high levels of social trust increase nonviolent discipline? Two potential explanations emerge. In his landmark work on the power of nonviolent action, Gregg (2018) discussed the "moral jiu-jitsu" of remaining nonviolent even when a government engages in violent repression. Gregg argued that by eschewing violent action, participants in civil resistance campaigns can invoke in their opponents the moral quandary of engaging in violent action against nonviolent challengers. Here, Uslaner's (2002) moral conception of trust is central: civil resistance activists and organizations conceive of a moral community as encompassing not just activists and organizations within the civil resistance campaign, but also members of the government regime. Moreover, it suggests that they believe government agents share that belief of the moral community. Operating from this framework, one would expect that high-trusting individuals would be less likely to justify the use of violent action for political gain than lower-trusting individuals.

Alternatively, trust may serve as a cohesive force within a civil resistance organization or campaign that is engaged in anti-government action. For the potential activist in Africa, social trust may play a critical role in driving expectations about whether a civil resistance movement can, in fact, remain committed to nonviolent action in the first place. Scholars on trust have argued that social trust can decrease "the need for regulation by state and other institutions and [reduce] the transaction and monitoring costs of ordinary spontaneous relationships" (Cook, Hardin, and Levi 2005, 1). Thus, when an individual considers whether to join a nonviolent movement, higher levels of social trust are likely to reassure her about the commitment of the organization to nonviolent principles. This is particularly important in the African context, where political violence is common and governments have often struggled to enforce basic social order.

Trust may serve to maintain nonviolent discipline in times of procedural or strategic uncertainty. In environments where newly mobilized activists are unsure of how much they can trust their new acquaintances, they may be less able or willing to maintain and enforce nonviolent discipline than in environments where they trust that their voices will be heard. Activists committed to nonviolent action may be unsure how much they can trust the commitment of their fellow participants to uphold standards of nonviolent action.[21] Group norms, such as the commitment to nonviolent action, are more likely to be violated in thinner social networks (Booth, Farrell, and Varano 2008; Hirschi 1969). In low-trust, spontaneous events, group leaders are less able to sanction violent behavior (Chaurand and Brauer 2008). Recent research has shown that nonviolent protests are more likely to retain nonviolent discipline in the presence of clear leadership hierarchies (Ives and Lewis 2020). While many civil resistance organizations are professional and campaigns are well-coordinated, this is not always the case. For example, the civil resistance campaigns that rocked North Africa and the Middle East beginning in 2010 emerged out of what were initially unstructured networks rather than highly organized labor unions or church or mosque groups (Tufekci 2017). In such

---

21 Consider the behavior of Black Bloc anarchists, who often infiltrate nonviolent protests in order to deliberately engage in violent disruption (Africa Research Bulletin 2013). These individuals are able, with a small cohort of provocateurs, to derail meaningful peaceful protests, altering the ability of activists to frame their movement as civil resistance.

circumstances, high levels of social trust may help reduce the onset of violent action by altering how participants perceive their circumstances. For example, new activists that are committed to nonviolent civil resistance and are operating in a high-trust environment may be less likely to believe themselves to be in a potentially violent situation (Collins 2008), particularly if they trust that their fellow activists will maintain nonviolent discipline. In this sense, trust is seen as a guarantee that participants will observe and maintain group norms of nonviolent action.

Furthermore, there is reason to believe that once an activist has joined a civil resistance organization, high levels of trust should correspond with nonviolent discipline. Within organizations, trust may substitute for direct oversight of the behavior of other members. In other words, the more trust found within an organization, the less need there is to audit the behavior of members. This in turn may generate a culture of trust and nonviolent civil resistance in which activists sense that the norms of nonviolent action are strongly upheld and unquestioned within the organization.

Studying nonviolent discipline (and transitions to nonviolent action) has generally been conducted at the level of the organization or campaign in civil resistance settings (Butcher and Svensson 2016; Véronique Dudouet 2013; Pinckney 2016). This approach has provided important insights into the structural and group-level characteristics that support nonviolent discipline, but it does not address the preferences of individuals who may mobilize within those groups. Work by Ives and Lewis (2020) has emphasized the importance of such "violence-oriented actors" in their theory of contentious gatekeeping. Thus, this monograph seeks to examine nonviolent discipline at the level of individual preferences for nonviolent or violent action. Doing so may provide key insights into the micro-level psychology that helps to shape civil resistance organizations and campaigns.

Prediction 2: High levels of social trust correspond with lower justifications for the use of violent action or observed violent action.

Expectations for This Study

In summary, this study seeks to understand how social trust may shape the willingness of individuals to participate in nonviolent protests as well as their justifications for the use of violent action. It makes two basic predictions. First, it predicts that individuals that have high levels of social trust, which will be approximated using several measurements, should be more likely to state that they are willing to participate in a protest. This is referred to as *potential mobilization*. Second, it predicts that individuals with high levels of social trust, again approximated using a variety of measurements, should express lower justification for violent action. The next two chapters are devoted to testing these predictions.

Chapter 2: Trust and Participation in Nonviolent Protest

This chapter focuses on testing the first prediction that high levels of social trust encourage the potential mobilization in a nonviolent resistance action, namely nonviolent protest. The second prediction—that high levels of social trust improve nonviolent discipline—is tested in the following chapter. Most statistical terms and tables can be found in the statistical appendix. This chapter uses statistical analysis to test whether high levels of social trust correspond with increased willingness to mobilize and participate in nonviolent protests, drawing primarily from survey data collected from across Africa over a 20-year period. This study finds initial support that high levels of social trust do correspond to an increased willingness to participate in nonviolent protests. It is then tested whether this willingness—which is referred to as *potential mobilization*—corresponds to actual nonviolent mobilization that occurred in the region. The results indicate that they do.

Model and Data

In order to test whether trust shapes nonviolent mobilization, evidence is drawn from the Afrobarometer surveys (2019). The Afrobarometer project is an extensive survey data project that collects nationally representative data across multiple African countries. This survey project has collected seven rounds of data from 1999 to 2019. These rounds operate similarly to a census—researchers knock on the doors of randomly-selected households and ask questions about a wide range of topics. The data include a wide variety of questions, including demographic information, political and economic views, and perceptions and experience with corruption. Importantly, the questionnaires have often included questions on different forms of trust and willingness to participate in protests, rallies, and other events. As such, the Afrobarometer dataset provides an excellent foundation upon which to build an analysis of the relationship between trust and mobilization.

There are limitations to the data, however. Unfortunately, not all questions are found on all rounds. For example, despite seven rounds existing, only rounds 3 through 5 include direct measurements of social trust. While this limits the ability of this analysis to study changes in the trust–protest relationship over time, the large sample of respondents found in each round remains robust enough to draw meaningful conclusions about the relationship between trust and willingness to protest. Table 1. Observations in Afrobarometer Rounds 3–5 displays the total number of observations in each round below.

Table 1. Observations in Afrobarometer Rounds 3–5

	ROUND 3	ROUND 4	ROUND 5
Number of respondents	25,397	27,713	51,587

In an ideal world, scholars prefer to examine *causal relationships*. By this, the monograph refers to the way in which one important **input** will *cause* a change in an **outcome**. Even though this study would like to test whether *higher or lower levels of trust cause mobilization and/or adherence to nonviolent discipline*, it cannot test directly the causality because the data found in the Afrobarometer are what is known as observational data. In short, this means that the data are recorded as they naturally occur rather than being controlled in some manner by the researcher.

In this monograph, the study instead presents *correlational relationships*, which are able to show how one input factor (such as social trust) relates to an outcome (such as participation in nonviolent protest). While correlational analyses cannot test more definitive claims about causal impact, they do provide an enormous benefit to scholars and activists alike. Correlational analysis can help demonstrate robust relationships between important social phenomena and can be analyzed in depth to suggest (though, not prove) causal pathways. Because the vast majority of data used in the social sciences are *observed* (that is, recorded by a third party after the fact), the bulk of social science research relies on correlational analysis.

The first expected outcome speaks to the willingness of individuals to participate in civil resistance actions. There is a wide portfolio of actions that civil resistance activists and groups may use. Gene Sharp (1973) identified 198 nonviolent actions that could be employed in pursuit of civil resistance. While the Afrobarometer dataset does not ask about each of these, it does ask about a common nonviolent act found within the portfolio of civil resistance: namely, participation in assemblies of protest. Thus, the outcome for the first set of tests is the willingness expressed by Afrobarometer respondents to engage in a protest, or *potential mobilization*.[22] Respondents were presented with "a list of actions that people sometimes take as citizens," including whether they had "[a]ttended a demonstration or protest march." Responses are recorded on a five-point scale. On one side of the scale is the response that

---

22 Importantly, levels of reported willingness to engaged in a protest—or even self-reported experience engaging in protests—likely differ from actual mobilization behavior. Socially desirable response bias, a form of misreporting commonly found in surveys, describes how survey respondents will select answers that they believe to be most socially acceptable, regardless of whether they accurately reflect the truth (Ansolabehere and Hersh 2012; Steenkamp, De Jong, and Baumgartner 2010). This is a challenge when examining whether reported willingness to engaged in protests or other political behavior correlates with actual participation if and when the time for such action arises. Due to limitations with the data, this study can only examine whether increased levels of trust shape *reported willingness to participate in protests*, which is referred to as *potential mobilization*. This is tested later in the chapter.

an individual has never and would never protest. On the other side is the response that an individual frequently participates in protests.

Figure 2. Willingness to Attend a Protest displays the proportion of responses to the question of protest participation. The majority of Africans report that they have never taken part in a protest, with 56.73 percent indicating that they would never do so. 28.95 percent of respondents indicate that they have not, but would do so if they had the chance. The remaining 11.6 percent of Africans state that they have engaged in a protest at least once. While this may seem low, it is important to remember that scholarship in civil resistance has indicated that successful civil resistance merely needs 3.5 percent of a population to become regularly engaged in a civil resistance campaign (Chenoweth 2013).

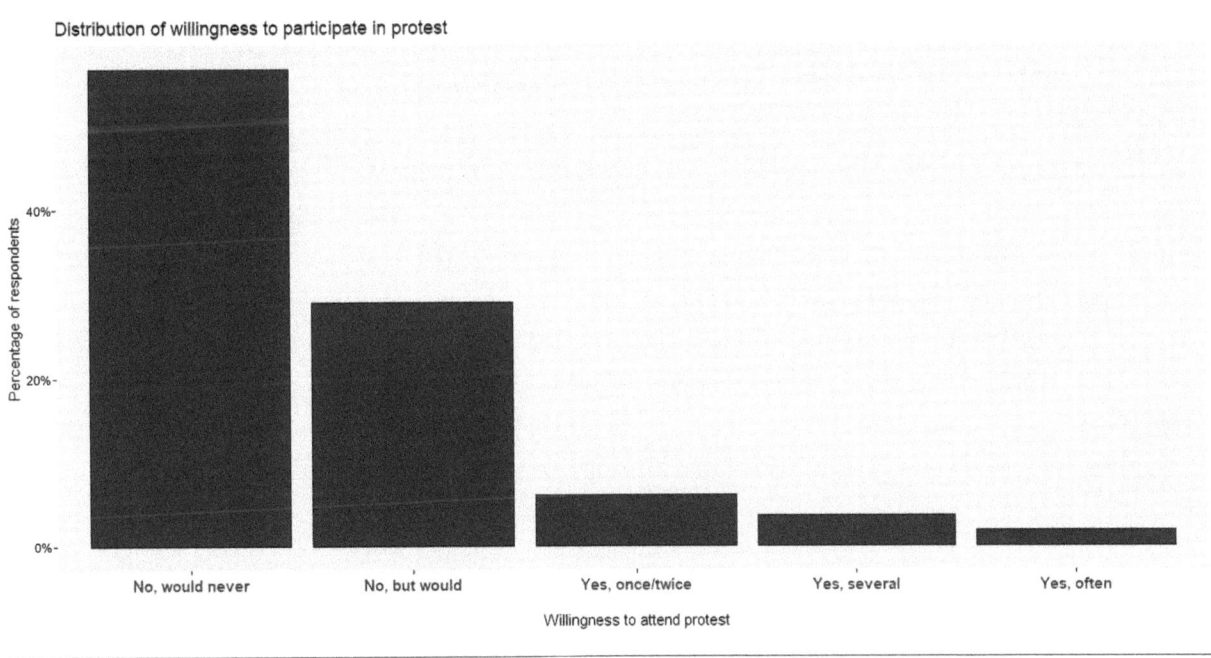

FIGURE 2. Willingness to Attend a Protest

In order to test the relationship between social trust and potential mobilization, this monograph draws from multiple measurements of trust that are found within the Afrobarometer dataset in order to sketch out the most robust possible relationship. The first two measurements are the most broad. The first question asks, "Generally speaking, would you say that most people can be trusted or that you must be very careful in dealing with people?" Respondents can answer either "you must be very careful" or "most people can be trusted." This is referred to as generalized social trust and is defined in the previous chapter. This question was asked in the third (2005–2006) and fifth (2011–2013) rounds. In total, 83 percent of Africans responded that one "must be very careful," indicating very low levels of social trust. For example, in Lesotho in 2011–2013 over 94 percent of respondents reported that one "must be very careful," with only 5.2 percent of respondents affirming that "most people can be trusted." Because this measurement of trust includes only two potential responses—and because they are relatively extreme—this measurement offers a very extreme view of trust.[23] To address this, the study turns to another, more granular measurement. The second measure of social trust focuses on trust in fellow citizens of the respondent's country. This question is found only in round 4, which was collected from 2005 to 2006. Respondents were asked, "Let's turn to your views on your fellow citizens. How much do you trust each of the following types of people? Other [nationality]." Respondents were allowed to pick from the following responses: "not at all," "just a little," "somewhat," or "a lot." This measurement of trust is referred to as *co-national trust*.

The third measure of social trust is of one's neighbors. The question is worded: "How much do you trust each of the following types of people: your neighbors?" Like the question concerning trust in fellow co-nationals, the scale measures from "not at all" to "a lot." *Trust in one's neighbors* is a peculiar measurement because, while many individuals may not be able to choose their neighbors, they do come into frequent contact with them. The scholarship on trust speaks to this complicated relationship, and many studies have shown that individuals living in highly diverse neighborhoods exhibit low levels of social trust.[24] Most of these studies, however, have been conducted in European countries where the state is able to provide basic social goods; in many African contexts, citizens rely more heavily on their informal social networks, including their neighbors, in order to attain social support and secure basic goods. Trust in one's neighbors is found in rounds 3 and 5 of the Afrobarometer data.

The most intimate measure of social trust is of one's acquaintances. The question is phrased as such: "Let's turn to your views on your fellow citizens. How much do you trust each of the following types of people? Other people you know." This is referred to as *trust in acquaintances*. The same response scale that applied to the question on fellow citizens and neighbors applies to this question. Unlike the measures of fellow citizens and neighbors, this measurement indexes how one trusts acquaintances. Speaking of "other people you know" is still vague, but it is reasonable to assume that most people interpret this to refer to people within one's social circle. This measurement is thus subject to a selection effect: we tend to associate with people that we like or with whom we work, attend religious services, or otherwise agree with. Despite this selection effect, this measurement is included because it improves the thoroughness of the analysis.

---

23 When compared to a measurement of trust that uses a scale, for example, that allows respondents to state that they have "a lot" of trust, "some trust," or "no trust at all."

24 For more information on this, see Sonderskov (2011a).

Descriptive Evidence

We begin with an initial descriptive analysis of the Afrobarometer data. Such a descriptive approach can show the basic relationship between social trust and potential mobilization, but it does not factor in other potential issues, such as respondent gender, economic conditions, and other important factors to take into consideration. These are included later in the statistical analysis. Figure 3. Different Measurements of Social Trust and Reported Potential Mobilization displays the relationship between each of the four forms of trust discussed earlier in this monograph and the willingness of respondents to join a nonviolent protest or demonstration.

The bottom horizontal axis of each plot tracks levels of trust. On the left of each plot are those with no trust at all in their fellow citizens, neighbors, and acquaintances. The vertical axis measures the average level of respondents to join a protest. Worryingly, the top-left plot suggests a relatively strong and negative relationship between generalized social trust and potential mobilization. As discussed further below, this may be due to the way that the question is structured. It is also worth noting that this negative relationship reverses when the respondents who indicate that they *would never* attend a protest are exempted from analysis; thus, of those individuals who are not completely opposed to engaging in protest, increases in generalized social trust actually increases potential mobilization substantially.

The top-right plot provides initial support for the expected outcome that higher trust in one's co-nationals corresponds with greater levels of potential mobilization. What is evident is that individuals with higher levels of generalized trust in their fellow citizens are increasingly likely to respond that they would at least be willing to join a nonviolent protest and (in many cases) that they already have. In the bottom-left plot, trust in one's neighbors seems to be inversely related to the willingness to engage in protest. This runs counter to expectations

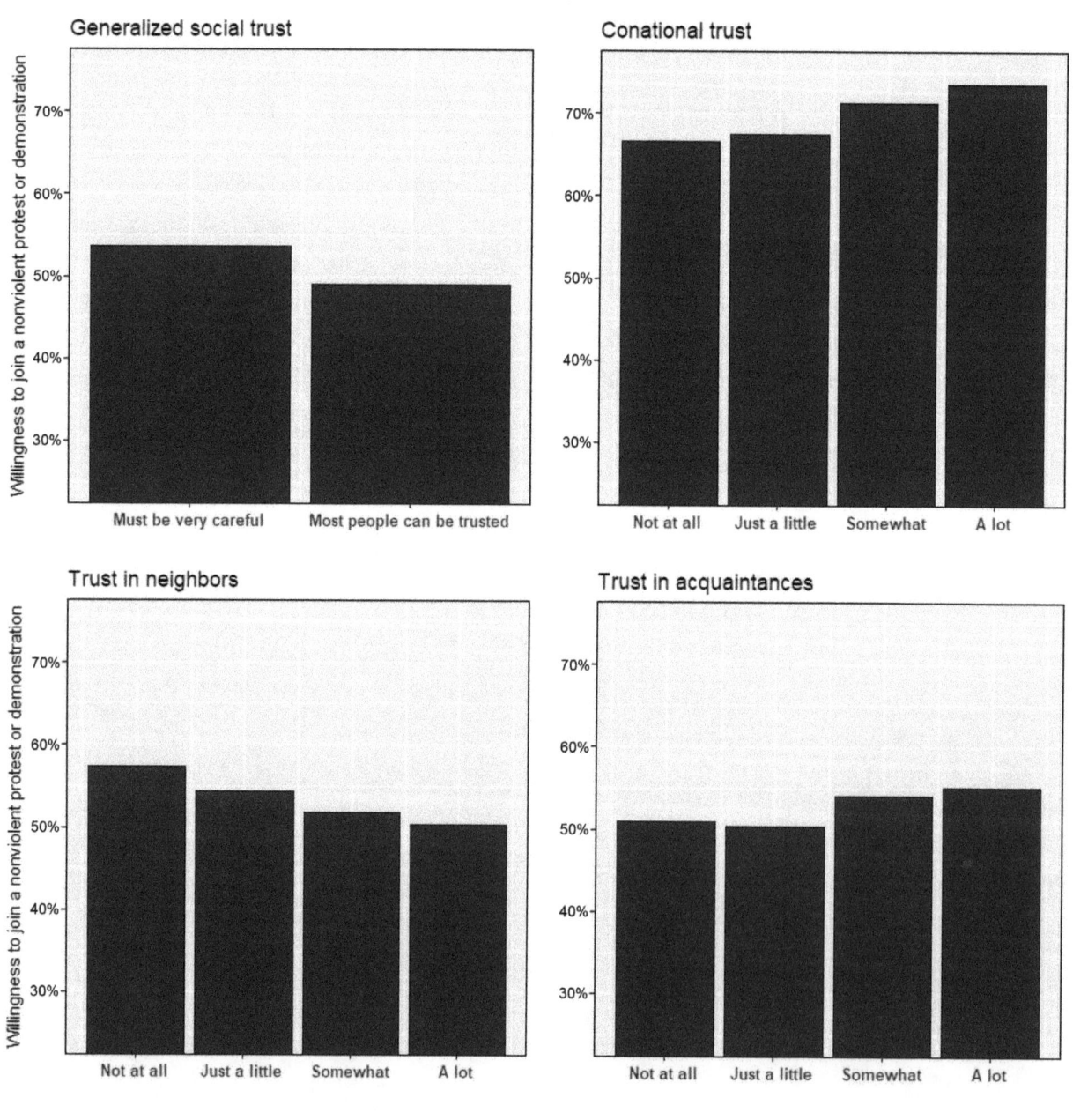

FIGURE 3. Different Measurements of Social Trust and Reported Potential Mobilization

and adds complexity to the overall argument. This demonstrates the importance of approaching and analyzing trust with nuance. Why might trust in neighbors correspond with less willingness to potentially mobilize? An in-depth analysis is beyond the scope of this study; however, one potential explanation may be due to the demographic composition of neighborhoods. If neighborhoods are composed of ethnically or religiously homogenous groups of people, then a question about trust in one's neighbors may actually be a question about trust in one's ethnic or religious group. Finally, the bottom-right plot shows that as trust in one's acquaintances increases, so does the reported willingness to engage in protests.

Statistical Model

Having examined the data at their face value, the study now turns to the use of statistical models in order to more accurately estimate the relationship between different forms of trust and willingness to mobilize in a protest. Thus far, the analysis has considered only the relationship between two factors: trust and mobilization. But, of course, these are not the only factors that matter. In this section, the components of the statistical model are briefly described to further and more robustly test the proposed relationship by accounting for alternative factors described below. Information on the precise model specifications can be found in the statistical appendix.

The statistical model is *hierarchical*, incorporating information about which country each respondent is from. In order to make the model more accurate, the analysis includes several important factors to minimize the likelihood of omitted variable bias. For example, the models include the gender of the respondent as a standard measure that is often used in survey research. Additionally, age likely shapes whether someone is willing to engage in protests, which are often physically demanding and involve marching and the threat of repression from the state. The analysis also includes a measurement of each respondent's perceptions of the current economic status of the country. Substantial work has demonstrated that economic perceptions shape protest and contentious mobilization (Mampilly 2011; Mueller 2013, 2018) and it is important to include such information in any analysis of protest intention. Along a similar line, the analysis includes a measurement that measures a respondent's relative living situation. One major line of research in conflict studies focuses on what Gurr called "relative deprivation" (Gurr 1970). Many scholars[25] have built on this school of thought, which argues that the impetus to mobilize is linked to perceptions of one's material deprivation relative to others in society. The models also include an indicator of the level of education that each respondent has attained. Respondents with higher educational attainment are likely

---

25   Stewart (2010) and others (Cederman, Weidmann, and Gleditsch 2011; Østby 2008) have taken great efforts to extend Gurr's thesis to apply to groups within society rather than individuals.

more aware of political issues and thus more likely to be aware of potential civil resistance opportunities. Finally, the models include three measurements of perceived corruption. Government corruption is a major and highly salient issue in African politics, and recent work has shown that it can motivate participation in protests (Auyero 2003; Beyerle 2014; Johnston 2005; Lewis 2020). Many civil resistance movements have recently included corruption as a central grievance in their claims against the government (Alexander 2010; Beyerle 2014; Evelyne Musambi 2018; Security 2019). These measurements include perceptions of corruption of the president, the parliament, and the police.

Results

The results demonstrate mixed findings. Two of the four measurements of trust (trust in fellow citizens and trust in acquaintances) provide relatively strong support for the expectation that social trust positively relates to potential mobilization,[26] while the other two behave counter to expectations. Table 2. Results for Trust and Potential Mobilization Using the Full Sample summarizes the overall results of the statistical tests. Trust in co-nationals—a very broad measure of social trust—corresponds very strongly with potential mobilization. Even holding other factors constant—such as age, gender, and economic views— there is a robust and positive relationship between how much people claim they trust their fellow compatriots and their reported willingness to participate in a protest or demonstration. According to the test, respondents with high levels of trust in their fellow citizens score 5 percent higher than low-trust individuals in their stated willingness to mobilize by joining a protest or demonstration. Respondents with high trust in their acquaintances score just over 6 percent higher in potential mobilization.

Table 2. Results for Trust and Potential Mobilization Using the Full Sample

TRUST MEASUREMENT	STATISTICAL RELATIONSHIP	MEETS EXPECTATIONS?
Generalized social trust	Negative, not significant	No
Trust in co-nationals	Positive, significant	Yes
Trust in neighbors	Negative, not significant	No
Trust in acquaintances	Positive, significant	Yes

Generalized social trust does not demonstrate much of a relationship at all and is not statistically significant. This may be due to the way in which the question is structured.[27]

---

26   The results can be found in Table 7 in the statistical appendix.

27   Unlike the other questions on trust, this question asks respondents whether they believe that either most people can be trusted or whether they have to be very careful in dealing with them. The wording of this question is both vague (i.e., what does it mean that one has to be very careful?) and ominous. Moreover, because there are only two responses, the question doesn't capture any gradation in levels of trust.

Perhaps most surprising is the finding that respondents with high levels of trust in their neighbors are less likely to report a willingness to potentially mobilize. One additional consideration is that the data skew heavily toward respondents stating that they would never consider mobilizing. It is not possible in this study to evaluate whether this response truly channels hostility toward participating in protests and demonstrations or whether it reflects other considerations. For example, in low trust environments, respondents may not be willing to reveal their true preferences for potential mobilization.

The statistical analysis provides an additional benefit to civil resistance organizations seeking to recruit new activists: a cross-country analysis of where the relationship between trust and potential mobilization is strongest and where it is weakest. Across the board, the tests indicate that several countries stand out. Ghana, Togo, and Mali—all West African countries with relatively stable democracies—consistently report strong, positive relationships between social trust and potential mobilization. Interestingly, Sudan and Algeria—two countries that regularly display negative and significant relationships—had largely nonviolent and successful civil resistance campaigns in 2019. This suggests that trust may be most strongly related to civil resistance activity (including protests) when channeled through existing networks, such as labor unions, religious organizations, and student groups. For example, the Sudanese civil resistance movement was populated by student organizations calling for an end to al-Bashir's rule (Rashwan 2019b).[28] For civil resistance organizations seeking to mobilize new activists, the results provide empirical evidence for what they likely already suspect: recruiting potential activists from high-trust networks is likely to be successful.

The results in this chapter demonstrate that there is a positive relationship between how much an individual trusts his or her fellow citizens or acquaintances and his or her reported willingness to engage in protests. Of course, reported willingness and actual willingness are not the same, and thus the latter half of this chapter is dedicated to studying the relationship between the two. But on the whole, civil resistance organizations would be smart to tap into existing high-trust networks. These could include religious organizations, civic organizations, or student networks, to name a few.

In addition to these main findings, several other findings stand out:

1. **Economic evaluations are not consistently linked to protest**. Running counter to traditional explanations found in both the scholarship on protest politics (Alexander 2010; Lancaster 2018; Mueller 2013), this suggests that while "pocketbook protesting"[29]

---

28 For more on the role of existing networks and mobilization in Sudan's nonviolent revolution, see the ICNC Special Report, *Sudan's 2019 Revolution: The Power of Civil Resistance* by Stephen Zunes. **https://www.nonviolent-conflict.org/resource/sudans-2019-revolution-the-power-of-civil-resistance/**.

29 "Pocketbook protesting" refers to the mobilization of protests around economic issues.

may be important, it is not the only factor that motivates individuals to rise up or participate. Work specifically on civil resistance has arrived at mixed conclusions. Some scholars argue that economic concerns are not determinants of either mobilization or success (Chenoweth and Stephan 2011; Zunes 2017), though others have found that economic decline can generate mass mobilization against regimes (Larmer 2009; LeBas 2011). This remains an open question meriting further study.

2. **Education is consistently linked with activism**. Across every model, individuals with higher levels of education on the African continent are more likely to indicate that they are at least willing to engage in a protest. In part, this is likely due to an increased awareness of government corruption and human rights abuses. It also likely links to the willingness of students to regularly engage in mass mobilization (Dahlum and Wig 2020; Nyadu and Twala 2017). Across Africa, student organizations have played major roles in nonviolent and primarily nonviolent resistance campaigns, including the National Union of South African Students (Thompson 2014, 205), student protesters in Sudan's recent civil resistance campaign (Rashwan 2019b), and nonviolent student action in Zimbabwe calling for former president Robert Mugabe's resignation (Graham-Harrison 2017).

3. **Perceptions of presidential corruption are linked with potential mobilization**. Across every model, respondents that believe that the president of their country is corrupt are significantly more likely to report that they would be willing to attend a nonviolent protest or demonstration.[30] This is consistent with observed civil resistance movements across Africa since the second wave of protest in the 1990s; corrupt governments are illegitimate (Mendilow and Peleg 2016; Rotberg 2003) and often engage in anti-democratic behaviors in order to protect their access to wealth and power. Whether throughout North Africa during the Arab Spring or more recently throughout Sub-Saharan Africa, corruption has regularly been a major claim made by civil resistance organizations seeking to transition to or improve the quality of their democracy.

Does Potential Mobilization Correlate with Actual Mobilization?

This research has thus far focused on testing whether heightened social trust corresponds with the willingness of respondents to actually mobilize and participate in nonviolent protests. The question of the validity of self-reported political and social behavior has been scrutinized

---

30   Most African nations are majoritarian presidential systems in which presidents yield substantial power over the political system and the distribution of state resources. Thus, presidential corruption is of major concern to most citizens of African countries. This has been demonstrated by Lewis (2020).

heavily—after all, citizens may feel inclined to respond to survey questions in ways that conform to social pressures.[31] They may also respond to surveys in ways that reflect how they wish they had behaved rather than how they actually behaved, particularly in contentious actions that also carry a degree of risk. Work by Andersson and Granberg (1997) found that in high trust contexts,[32] Swedish citizens reported their voting behavior with relative honesty. Of course, in most African contexts, levels of trust are substantially lower than in Sweden, and there are added concerns about intimidation and exposure to violence. Research on the relationship between attitudes toward protest have shown tentative evidence that when respondents have positive attitudes toward political protest, they are more likely to engage in prosocial political actions (Sweetman et al. 2019). This work supports recent work by McClendon and Riedl (2015), who found that in Kenya, the experimental manipulation of how people view themselves can increase political participation.

These studies provide initial evidence that measuring potential mobilization can indeed provide important insight into how Africans may actually behave. In this section of the chapter, the study builds on this by examining whether high levels of reported potential mobilization correspond to observed levels of nonviolent protest behavior across Africa. Drawing from the Afrobarometer data, the average reported potential mobilization for each country was calculated for each survey round. Most countries were surveyed in multiple years, which provides the opportunity to examine the rise or fall of reported potential mobilization within a single country over time.[33] Average reported potential mobilization was calculated via the mathematical average of all responses about one's willingness to attend a protest (on a scale from 0 to 4). A response indicating that someone has not engaged in protest and would never do so receives a value of 0, whereas a response indicating that someone often engages in protest receives a value of 4.

For the fifth round of surveys in Algeria from 2013, the average reported level of potential mobilization is 0.220. This is rather low, and during 2013, Algeria experienced 105 nonviolent protests.[34] In 2015, Algerians were once again surveyed. When asked about their willingness to protest, they reported an average potential mobilization of 0.616—nearly three-fold their

---

[31] Work in survey research has identified what has come to be called "social desirability bias," in which respondents claim to have behaved in ways that they believe conform with social norms (Steenkamp, De Jong, and Baumgartner 2010). In these cases, respondents might claim to have voted when they did not, overreport their contributions to charity, or claim to have engaged in historic protests when they did not.

[32] In this case, Sweden.

[33] Unlike the initial analysis, which was limited to rounds 3 through 5, this analysis does not rely on variables of trust. Fortunately, the potential mobilization variable can be found in rounds 2 through 7, expanding the ability to examine variation in the relationship between potential and actual mobilization over time.

[34] Observed via the Armed Conflict Location Event Data (Raleigh et al. 2010).

potential mobilization score from two years prior. In 2015, Algeria experienced 240 nonviolent protests—more than twice the protests than in 2013. Similarly, in Nigeria in 2013, respondents reported an average potential mobilization of 0.38 with a total of 273 observed protests. Two years later, potential mobilization increased to 0.76, and observed protests increased to 545. In 2017, Nigerians reported a very slight decrease in potential mobilization (0.74) and observed a slight decrease in protests (484).

Figure 4. Potential and Actual Mobilization visualizes the overall relationship between self-reported potential mobilization and observed levels of mobilization across Africa. It includes every survey round and every country in the Afrobarometer dataset. According to the data, the average potential mobilization score across all countries and all years is 0.59, and the majority of potential mobilization scores fall within a "normal range" between 0.38 and 0.80.[35] Figure 4. Potential and Actual Mobilization includes four bars that represent observed potential mobilization within and outside of this range. The leftmost bar displays the average number of nonviolent protests in countries where potential mobilization falls below the normal range of potential mobilization. In countries that reported very low potential mobilization—that is, potential mobilization that falls below the normal range—there was an average of 33 protests. The middle two bars ("low potential" and "medium potential") fall within the normal range. Low potential refers to the lower half of the range and medium potential refers to the upper half of that range. In low potential countries, there was an average of 70 observed nonviolent protests. In medium potential countries, there was an average of 76 nonviolent protests. Finally, the rightmost bar represents those countries that reported higher levels of potential mobilization, falling above the range. In these countries, there was an average of 78 observed nonviolent protests. Overall, the analysis provides initial support that potential mobilization and actual mobilization are linked.

Figure 4. Potential and Actual Mobilization suggests an unexpected relationship. When countries report potential mobilization either within or above the normal range, there is a small, positive relationship between self-reported potential mobilization and actual observed mobilization. Holding all else constant, the model predicts that if a country increased its potential mobilization from "low potential" to "highest potential," it would experience nearly 10 additional observed protests. This is helpful in making strides toward understanding the relationship between potential and actual mobilization, but not conclusive—and it is important to recognize that many factors play a role in determining whether citizens are willing to mobilize. On the left-hand side of the plot, however, there is a sharp drop-off in observed protests in the countries with the lowest levels of potential mobilization. The data thus suggest that this relationship is conditioned by other, more important factors, perhaps including political

---

35 Calculated using standard deviations. The distribution of potential mobilization is not distributed perfectly normally and is slightly bimodal.

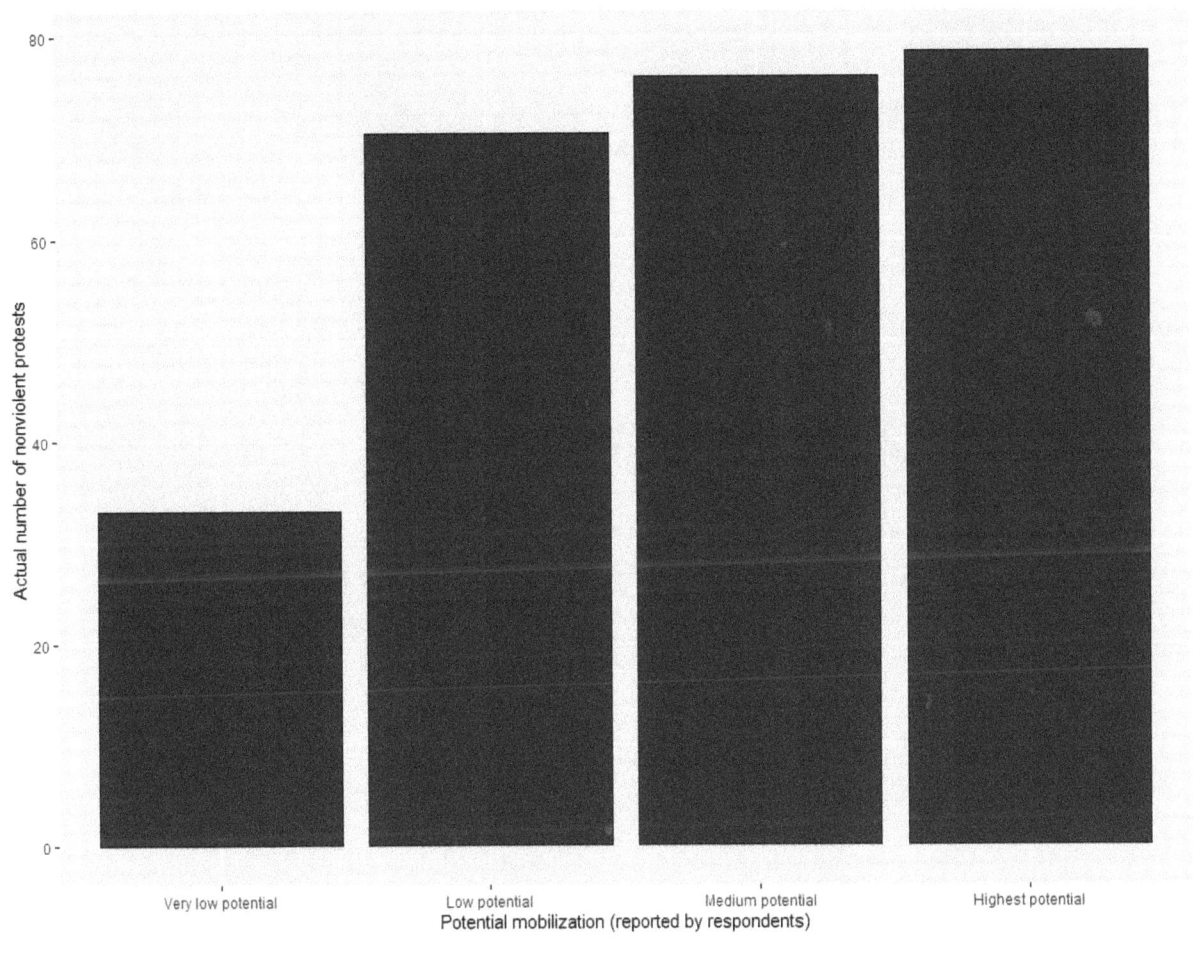

FIGURE 4. Potential and Actual Mobilization

stability, internal security, and levels of democracy. In many cases, respondents may be concerned that indicating that they would consider mobilizing could result in their being targeted by the government for repression. Additional research on the relationship between these factors and social trust is merited.

Furthermore, it seems to be that the relationship between potential mobilization and actual mobilization is most visible within countries rather than across countries. Rises in potential mobilization do seem to correlate with rises in actual mobilization within a country, but it is not particularly helpful to compare across countries. As mentioned above, citizens in some countries are subject to substantially more intense government scrutiny and repression than in other countries. In relatively free, fair, and well-governed countries, it makes intuitive sense that citizens would simultaneously feel free to protest without feeling the need to protest. In other countries, citizens may feel the need to protest but not feel free to do so. Thus, by analyzing variation within countries—and in particular, the countries in which protest might be most needed—the relationship between potential and actual mobilization is clearest. In Ghana and Morocco, for example, a rise in reported potential mobilization is accompanied by a rise in observed protests. This relationship does not always hold: in countries such as Kenya and Liberia, the relationship cuts the opposite way, with slight decreases in potential mobilization corresponding to a rise in observed mobilization. As a result, it is important that civil resistance organizations in different countries carefully consider many factors when deciding how to engage potential activists rather than simply assuming that citizens' expressed readiness to mobilize will directly lead to actual mobilization.

Summary of Chapter 2 Findings

What can be drawn from the evidence presented in this chapter? First, the results of the tests on social trust's relationship with potential mobilization tell an interesting, nuanced story. Four different measurements of social trust were used: trust in most other people, trust in acquaintances, trust in co-nationals, and trust in neighbors. These different measurements of trust were tested statistically against the potential willingness of citizens to participate in nonviolent protests and demonstrations. In two of the four tests, trust positively and significantly relates to potential willingness. When Africans report high levels of trust in either their personal acquaintances or their co-nationals, they are significantly more likely to state that they would be willing to engage in nonviolent protests or demonstrations.

After testing whether trust shapes potential mobilization, the study then turned to whether potential mobilization corresponds with actual mobilization by examining whether countries in which high levels of self-reported willingness to protest experience more protests than countries in which citizens report lower potential mobilization. The analysis suggests that there is reason to believe that citizens that report willingness to attend a protest or demonstration are indeed more likely to actually do so, though this relationship merits significantly more attention beyond the scope of this monograph.

Chapter 3: Trust and Nonviolent Action

In the previous chapter, this study used statistical tests that found that increased levels of social trust are positively related to the willingness of citizens to engage in nonviolent protests—or *potential mobilization*. It then tested whether potential mobilization corresponds to actual mobilization by evaluating whether regions with high levels of potential mobilization experience more nonviolent protests than regions with low levels of potential mobilization. The results suggest that this is the case, though they are not conclusive and merit further study. In this chapter, the study measures the impact of social trust on individual justifications for violent action. Civil resistance is considered most effective when individuals, groups, and campaigns maintain nonviolent discipline. While most civil resistance literature has focused on the nonviolent discipline of campaigns over time, this study instead examines justifications of violent action across Africa and then measures actual proportions of violent action in observed contentious events across the continent.

Nonviolent discipline has played a central role in many African resistance movements. While the anti-apartheid movement in South Africa fluctuated between violent and nonviolent resistance—though the struggle took a decisive turn to nonviolent resistance from the beginning of the 1980s—other campaigns such as the OccupyNigeria campaigns in 2012 (Hari 2014), the #StopTheseThieves anticorruption campaign in Kenya (Mariita 2018), the 2019 Sudanese Revolution (International Crisis Group 2019b), or the 2019 Algerian Revolution of Smiles have focused heavily on maintaining nonviolent discipline in order to maximize their effectiveness. Such nonviolent discipline is strategic, based on the general premise that civil resistance campaigns compete with governments to control the narrative and framing of the conflict. In this sense, a major battleground in any civil resistance campaign is that of the social narrative that surrounds and emanates from the campaign. A government that is seen as tyrannical and unjust may engender additional opposition (Gregg 2018; Sharp 2013). On the other hand, a civil resistance movement whose credentials and motives can be questioned may suffer from diminished legitimacy. For civil resistance movements, controlling the narrative very likely requires in-depth attention to the maintenance of nonviolent discipline. When civil resistance movements break their nonviolent discipline and turn to the use of violent tactics, this can have disastrous results on the ability to attract and mobilize support, as well as to control the conflict narrative (Chenoweth and Schock 2015).

Maintaining nonviolent discipline sends important signals about the intentions and structure of a civil resistance campaign. To observing citizens, civil resistance may reduce the perceived costs of mobilizing by minimizing the likelihood of repression. Citizens may believe that nonviolent campaigns are less likely to experience harsh violence at the hands of the state, or at least it is difficult for the regime to justify violence against unarmed and nonviolent demonstrators. Moreover, bystanders that are potentially interested in mobilizing but are on the fence may be more likely to assume lower costs of mobilization because they will not have to bypass any moral barriers that are required to engage in violent resistance. Additionally, remaining nonviolent sends a powerful signal of discipline to both bystanders and the government.

As detailed in Chapter 1, research on civil resistance has focused largely on nonviolent discipline at the organizational and campaign level. Research has shown that civil resistance campaigns become less likely to maintain nonviolent discipline when they represent large numbers of marginalized or excluded people (Rørbæk 2019), when campaigns include violence-oriented organizations (Ryckman 2020), and when campaigns are repressed by the government (Pinckney 2016). Butcher and Svensson (2016) draw upon theories of resource mobilization and argue that when resources can be mobilized through social networks that are economically interdependent or integrated with the state, organizations and movements should be more likely to maintain nonviolent discipline. Thus, when social networks produce goods or services that are consumed by the state, these networks find it in their interest to use nonviolent strategies that take advantage of such state's dependency on them. This interdependence thus fosters nonviolent discipline.

The study finds that such individuals with high levels of trust do indeed voice lower justifications for the use of violent action.

There has been less work that has focused on analyzing units smaller than campaigns. More recently, work centered on the event-level has shown that nonviolent protests may escalate toward reactive or unarmed violent action due to several factors. Ives and Lewis (2020) have shown that when the relative costs of the use of violent action to nonviolent action are low, protests may become violent. Sullivan (2018) has shown that when states have greater capacity to repress, events are more likely to turn violent. However, these studies overlook the relevance of individual-level preferences (that is, the preferences of individual activists) regarding violent or nonviolent action. This monograph draws upon individual-level data about justifications for violent action as an initial attempt to examine the relationship between trust and nonviolent discipline. Arguably, one central component of nonviolent discipline is when individuals within civil resistance organizations believe that violent political actions are unjustified. The views of individual activists toward whether violent action can ever be justified may shape the norms of civil resistance organizations, and thus when individuals reject violence outright, one should expect that this will be reflected in the ability of civil resistance organizations and campaigns to maintain nonviolent discipline.

Chapter 3 seeks to study the relationship between social trust and nonviolent discipline using two methods. First, this study turns again to the Afrobarometer data to test whether individuals with high levels of social trust are more likely to state that violent actions are never justified. While the Afrobarometer data do not include a question that directly asks respondents about their preferences toward nonviolent action, the data do include a question that asks about whether violent action can be justified. It is likely that individuals who believe that violent actions are never justified are more likely to hold preferences for nonviolent discipline than individuals who believe that violent actions are sometimes justifiable. It is expected that individuals who report higher levels of social trust will be more likely than low-trusting individuals to state that the use of violent action is never justified. This is an imperfect measurement in gauging preferences for nonviolent discipline, to be sure, and highlights the need for future research into the individual psychology of civil resistance activism. As such, this monograph should be considered a starting point rather than a final say on the relationship between social trust and preferences for nonviolent discipline. While a variable about justifications of violent action may not perfectly overlap with preferences for violent action, it does seem likely to be an acceptable proxy for it until a better measurement is produced.

This chapter produces two interesting results. First, drawing on the data mentioned above, the study finds that such individuals with high levels of trust do indeed voice lower justifications for the use of violent action. Second, it draws upon data of observed contentious politics (including nonviolent and violent actions) to test whether regions across Africa with higher levels of social trust experience higher proportions of nonviolent action than regions with lower levels of social trust. Relatively mixed findings are observed; the statistical relationship is often weak but suggests that higher levels of social trust correspond to higher proportions of nonviolent action. The results also indicate that regions with higher levels of trust in diverse populations (that is, trust in people from different ethnic groups) are more likely to experience nonviolent protests than regions with low levels of trust in diverse populations. Table 3. Expected Relationships Between Trust and Justification of Violent Action presents the expected relationship between trust and justification of violent action.

Table 3. Expected Relationships Between Trust and Justification of Violent Action

TRUST MEASUREMENT	EXPECTED RELATIONSHIP
Generalized social trust	Negative
Trust in diverse population	Negative
Trust in neighbors	Negative
Trust in acquaintances	Negative

Trust and Justification for Violent Action at the Individual Level

The study now returns to the Afrobarometer data to test the relationship between social trust and preferences for nonviolent action. Much like the initial tests in the previous chapter, the data are collected at the individual level, meaning that there are thousands of individual responses collected and analyzed. Of course, measuring support for violent actions is both difficult and sensitive, particularly on a continent where violence has often played a central role in politics. Asking individual respondents about their views on whether violent behavior is justified, then, is likely to produce highly biased statistics in which respondents overwhelmingly state that they are firmly against violence. After all, respondents are speaking to a stranger (the surveyor) who is asking them politically sensitive questions. In the Afrobarometer data, respondents were asked whether they agreed or strongly agreed with Statement A, "The use of violence is never justified," or Statement B, "It is sometimes necessary to use violence in support of a just cause."[36] The responses are visualized in Figure 5. Justification of Violent Action and confirm that the majority of respondents do indeed state that they agree strongly or agree that violence is never justified. In total, nearly 90 percent of all respondents agree or strongly agree that nonviolent action is always preferable to violent action and that violent action cannot be justified.

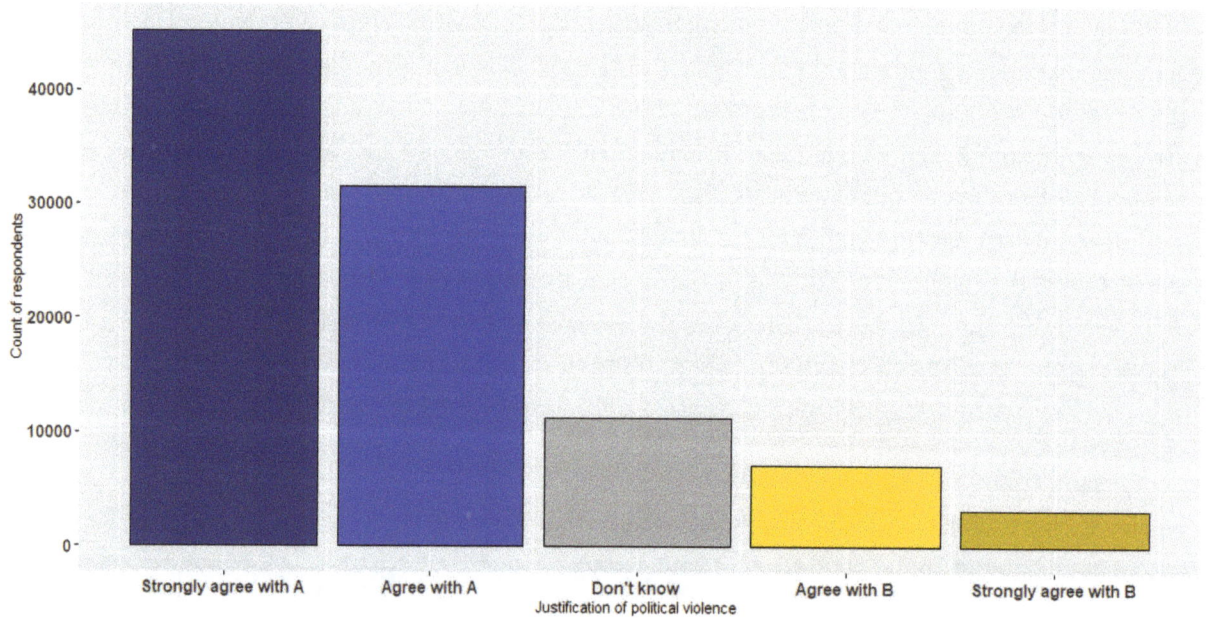

FIGURE 5. Justification of Violent Action

---

36 The wording of the survey includes "violence" as a noun rather than using violent as an adjective, such as "violent protest" or "violent riot."

In order to test the statistical relationship between high levels of social trust and justification for violent action, the same measurements of trust that were used in estimating how trust shapes potential mobilization are drawn upon. This includes the "most people can be trusted" measurement, the measurement about trust in one's neighbors, and the measurement of trust in one's acquaintances. Unfortunately, due to limitations with the data, the question measuring trust in one's fellow citizens is not available to test. Fortunately, there is a question that can serve as a substitute. It measures the respondent's level of trust in other fellow citizens who are not members of their ethnic group. The question is phrased as: "How much do you trust each of the following types of people: [fellow citizens] from other ethnic groups?" The monograph refers to this as "trust in diverse populations." The potential answers range from "not at all" to "a lot." This study includes this as a fourth measurement of social trust.

Model and Data

As with the examination of the impact of trust on mobilization, the analysis now tests the relationship more thoroughly using statistical models.[37] These models remain identical to those used earlier in this chapter and incorporate information about gender, evaluations of the country's present economic situation, evaluations of one's living conditions compared to others, levels of education, and age. Doing so allows the analysis to better estimate the actual relationship between these two different forms of trust and individual-level justifications for the use of violent actions in pursuit of political means.

Results

The results of the models provide support for the argument that high levels of trust correspond with lower justifications for violent action.[38] Of the four measurements of social trust, the strongest relationship is found in the measurement of non-ethnic fellow citizens. This means that respondents with high levels of trust in their non-ethnic fellow citizens are substantially more likely to state that violent actions are never justified than their low-trusting counterparts. This is a hopeful finding—it suggests that as social trust extends across ethnic groups, Africans become less tolerant of violence and perhaps more committed to nonviolent discipline as part of their contentious actions against a state. While this does not directly test the proposed trust relationship in the context of a multi-ethnic civil resistance campaign, examples such as South Africa's anti-Zuma mass mobilizations from 2015 to 2018 and Sudan's multi-ethnic challenge to Omar al-Bashir suggest that increasing trust in diverse populations may improve nonviolent discipline.

---

37 The details of the models can be found in Table 8 in the statistical appendix. For academics and policymakers, these details are well-worth reviewing as they provide important insight into the models.

38 See Table 10 in the statistical appendix.

The other measurements of trust also support this argument generally. Table 4. Results for Trust and Justifications of Violent Action presents all the results from the statistical tests. The only measurement of trust that is not found to be statistically related to justifications of violent action is the "most people can be trusted" measurement.

Table 4. Results for Trust and Justifications of Violent Action

TRUST MEASUREMENT	STATISTICAL RELATIONSHIP	MEETS EXPECTATIONS?
Generalized social trust	Negative, not significant	Mixed
Trust in diverse population	Negative, significant	Yes
Trust in neighbors	Negative, significant	Yes
Trust in acquaintances	Negative, significant	Yes

In order to better understand the findings, the monograph presents the predicted responses in Figure 6. Social Trust and Justifications of Violent Action. It is important to know that the measurement for justification of violent action is structured between 1 (the lowest value, indicating "strong support" that nonviolent action is the only justifiable action against the government) and 5 (the highest value, indicating "strong support" that violent action can sometimes be justified against the government). What one immediately notices is that the range of predictions is relatively constrained between 1.8 and 1.9. This means that even the least trusting of individuals, on average, agree or strongly agree that nonviolent action is the only justifiable method of resistance against the government. Because of this limited variation in predicted outcomes, it is relatively easy to calculate and contrast each measurement of trust's relationship with justifications for the use of violent action for political reasons. Within this scale, as individuals gain more trust (from lowest to highest) in their neighbors, acquaintances, and ethnically different co-nationals (referred to as "trust in diverse populations"), the models all predict that respondents are less willing to voice justification for the use of violent action. While the overall reductions seem small, it is worth remembering that the vast majority of respondents reported very low justification of violent action in the first place.

In addition to the main findings, several additional results emerge:

1. **Women are less likely to believe violent action is justified.** In three of the five models, female respondents are significantly less likely than their male counterparts to tolerate the use of violent tactics in pursuit of political goals. This suggests that civil resistance organizers should work to increase the number of women in their organizations and to include women's movements in the broader campaigns in order to maximize nonviolent discipline. In South Africa, for example, the Federation of South African Women and the Black Sash were highly organized women's movements that opposed apartheid using nonviolent tactics in the 1950s and 1960s (New York

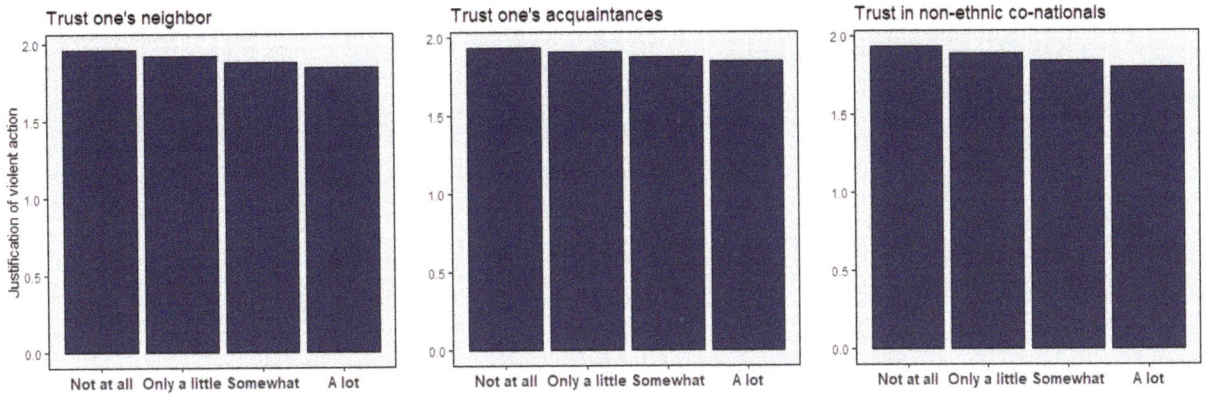

FIGURE 6. Social Trust and Justifications of Violent Action

Amsterdam News 2010; Thompson 2014). By broadening civil resistance movement goals to include gender equality, campaigns may be able to improve their ability to maintain nonviolent discipline.

2. **Highly educated respondents are less likely to believe violent action is justified.** In every model, higher levels of education correspond with reduced justification for violent action. Civil resistance movements should focus on providing a combination of civics education (for example, via the many tools provided by the International Center for Nonviolent Conflict) in tandem with civil resistance-focused training. By inspiring and educating current and future activists through civics education and the principles of nonviolent action, campaigns might be better able to remain nonviolent.

Trust and Observed Nonviolent Discipline

Thus far, the analysis in Chapter 3 has found that individuals who report high levels of social trust are more likely to state that they believe violent action is never justified. Yet, whether an individual is willing to justify the use of violent action is likely not a perfect proxy for commitment to nonviolent discipline. Testing the relationship between social trust and justifications for violent action provides some potential insight into how trust might shape nonviolent discipline, but additional evidence is required. To provide this additional evidence, the monograph now examines whether higher self-reported levels of trust correspond with higher proportions of nonviolent contention. If higher trust does indeed promote preferences for nonviolent action, then regions in which aggregate levels of trust are high should experience less violent action than regions in which aggregate levels of trust are low. Concordant with the theory presented earlier in this monograph, this study makes the prediction that in regions where citizens report high levels of social trust, there will be a higher percentage of nonviolent protest than in regions that report low levels of social trust.

There are mixed levels of support for this prediction. The analysis shows that increased levels of social trust do indeed correspond to higher proportions of nonviolent action; however, this relationship is contingent on the inclusion of several factors in the analysis, such as other forms of trust and other relevant factors. The tests provide suggestive support that the trust–nonviolent relationship does exist, though this requires more substantial research. The next section describes the data that were used to test the assumptions and presents the results in detail. As with the previous chapter, the majority of the statistical elements of analysis have been placed in Table 9 in the statistical appendix. The results of the tests are presented and the monograph explores not only generalized social trust but also delves into the role that trust in diverse populations (or "outgroup trust") plays in maintaining nonviolent discipline.

Model and Data

This monograph draws from the Armed Conflict Location Event Data (ACLED) as a source of protest and riot events. This dataset records observed incidents of many forms of conflict and contention; because this monograph focuses on civil resistance, observations were limited to include only protests and riots.[39] As with the Afrobarometer project, there are advantages and disadvantages to using these data. The major advantage is that the ACLED data are currently the most thorough collection of incidents of nonviolent protest and violent riots. Because nonviolent protests are a highly visible form of civil resistance, tapping into such a detailed dataset allows a clear and direct test of the prediction that high trust encourages nonviolent discipline. The disadvantage is that other forms of civil resistance action, such as speeches or refusal to cooperate, are not captured. This is a limitation of the data. However, because the ACLED data consist of nonviolent protests and violent riots, including both allows an evaluation of the proportion of overall contentious behavior that is nonviolent. The Afrobarometer data provides a nationally-representative snapshot of political sentiments in each country, and as such, this study correlates national levels of trust with the proportion of contentious events—often linked with civil resistance campaigns—that remain peaceful or transform nonviolent resistance into violent resistance.

The results presented in this chapter are correlational and rely on small sample sizes. As such, while they are able to provide insight into the relationship between levels of trust and levels of violent contention, they must be taken with a large grain of salt. Many factors have been shown to affect whether civil resistance campaigns and individual contentious incidents use peaceful or violent tactics. There is a large body of research detailing the impact of government repression

---

39   Other datasets, such as the Nonviolent and Violent Campaigns and Outcomes (NAVCO) 3 were considered. Because NAVCO 3 has a limited geographic scope and does not cover many African countries, it was not used.

on the increased use of violent tactics by formerly nonviolent protest movements and civil resistance campaigns (Ives and Lewis 2020; Nordas and Davenport 2013; Pinckney 2016; Sullivan 2018). Recent work has shown that civil resistance campaigns are more likely to break nonviolent discipline when large bodies of the population are excluded from political power along ethnic lines (Rørbæk 2019). This suggests that campaigns may be best served by developing and strengthening diverse networks that cross ethnic and religious lines, much like recent anti-corruption campaigns in South Africa and Kenya. In the language of trust, this suggests that civil resistance campaigns can best maintain nonviolent discipline by fostering high levels of trust in diverse ethnic networks.[40] Other work has demonstrated that campaigns with violent internal factions may fail to maintain nonviolent discipline (Ryckman 2020). This, too, suggests that trust may play an important role in cementing campaign norms and tactics and that the failure to build trust within campaigns can lead to factionalization and the possible emergence of violent flanks. The findings in this monograph further develop this line of inquiry by examining how social trust shapes the use of nonviolent strategies—specifically, nonviolent protest.

The goal of this section of the monograph is to answer the following question: in Africa, do regions where citizens report high levels of social trust experience a higher proportion of nonviolent protests or violent riots? By definition, only nonviolent protests can be counted from the large repertoire of civil resistance actions; however, in order to study whether higher trust corresponds with the maintenance of nonviolent discipline, it is necessary to compare nonviolent versus violent actions. One might ask, why not simply examine whether regions with high trust have *more nonviolent protests* than regions with low trust? The reason this would not work is that, quite naturally, some regions simply have more contentious actions than others. In a highly populated city, one should expect to see more protests than in a sparsely populated rural area. If this study only measured the number of protests between regions, it would falsely assume that nonviolent tactics are more popular in cities than in rural areas. Instead, it is important to look at the proportion of total observed protests and riots. This allows for a stronger comparison between regions: one can make meaningful comparisons between a region in which 25 percent of incidents are nonviolent protests and a region in which 75 percent are nonviolent.

---

40   Social psychologists focusing on Social Identity Theory (Tajfel and Turner 1986) speak of "ingroups" and "outgroups." Social Identity Theory is predicated on the premise that people conceive of social groups in which they consider themselves to be members. These groups reinforce sentiments of self-esteem and generate ingroup favoritism as well as outgroup bias. These groups may be developed along ethnic, linguistic, religious, or other lines. They also may be geographic, partisan, or based on other criteria (for instance, fans of the same sports team). Group memberships may overlap in some cases. Outgroups are the logical inverse of an ingroup—while ingroups are the categories of people to whom one considers themselves belonging, outgroups are categories of people to whom one does not consider themselves belonging. Work in political psychology has shown that we are much more likely to forgive the moral failings of our own ingroups while harshly punishing outgroups for similar infractions (Beber, Roessler, and Scacco 2014; Mackie and Ahn 1998; Raden 2003).

In order to analyze whether high levels of self-reported trust actually correspond with improved nonviolent action, two sources of data are connected: the self-reported levels of trust found in the Afrobarometer data and counts of nonviolent and violent contentious incidents found in the ACLED data. The Afrobarometer data are nationally-representative, individual-level surveys. The ACLED data, on the other hand, detail individual incidents of protest (nonviolent action) and riots (violent action). Thus, they had to be transformed in such a way as to speak to one another. In order to do this, the analysis used these two core datasets to generate three resultant datasets. The country-level dataset reports the average levels of reported trust[41] in each country. For instance, the average level of trust in Nigeria is calculated from all of the survey data collected in Nigeria from 2005 to 2015. Thus, each country receives only a single score for each form of trust. The disadvantage is that it collapses multiple years into a single value, which obscures variation in trust over time. This disadvantage is addressed in the next level of analysis.

The next level of analysis examines the average level of trust in each country but accounts for different rounds of the Afrobarometer data. The analysis includes rounds 3 through 6, which were collected in four data collection periods from 2005 through 2015. Table 5. Afrobarometer Rounds and Years displays the linkage between the Afrobarometer rounds and the years that they represent. Unfortunately, not all forms of trust are queried in each round, and not all rounds include the same countries. This creates discontinuities in the data that are unavoidable. Because the rounds correspond to specific years, protests and riots were coded to correspond with these years, creating a tighter linkage between self-reported levels of trust and incidents of violent and nonviolent actions.

Table 5. Afrobarometer Rounds and Years

ROUND 3	ROUND 4	ROUND 5	ROUND 6
2005–2006	2008–2009	2011–2015	2016–2018

The final level of analysis further disaggregates the data by recording the average levels of trust at the first administrative district level of each country per round. This is advantageous because it provides a tighter geographic connection between levels of trust and conflict. For example, levels of trust vary greatly from region to region in Nigeria. Not only that, but they do change over time. Trust is *sticky*, meaning that low-trust regions tend to remain as low-trust regions. But there is some meaningful variation, and this level of analysis is able to incorporate that variation. One limitation of this level of analysis is that the Afrobarometer data are not designed to be representative at the regional level. Therefore, one cannot make strong inferential claims about subnational levels of trust and contention.

---

41   Using each category of trust described in Chapter 2.

Protest events are considered nonviolent if they can reasonably be described as a peaceful protest, even if the protest was repressed by state forces. As long as the activists acted principally in accordance with nonviolent tactics, the incident is considered to have been peaceful. On the other hand, events are considered violent if they were described as either (a) mob violence or (b) a violent demonstration. This initial visualization of nonviolent and violent conflict at the country level provides evidence that there are important state-level factors that shape nonviolent discipline within different countries. In order to incorporate these country-level effects, this study uses the approach of examining variation within countries. Thus, the relationship between trust and nonviolent action within subnational regions are analyzed. This approach has two distinct advantages. First, it allows for the analysis of a specific subnational region (defined as the first administrative district within a country) over time. Thus, it is possible to test whether rising levels of social trust in Limpopo Province in South Africa lead to lower levels of violent anti-government action. This approach minimizes concerns about comparing trust and nonviolent action across different geographic regions, which may differ greatly from one another. Second, this allows for the comparison of different regions within the same country, which can reveal important information about how social trust may operate in some regions and not others. Within countries, there is often substantial

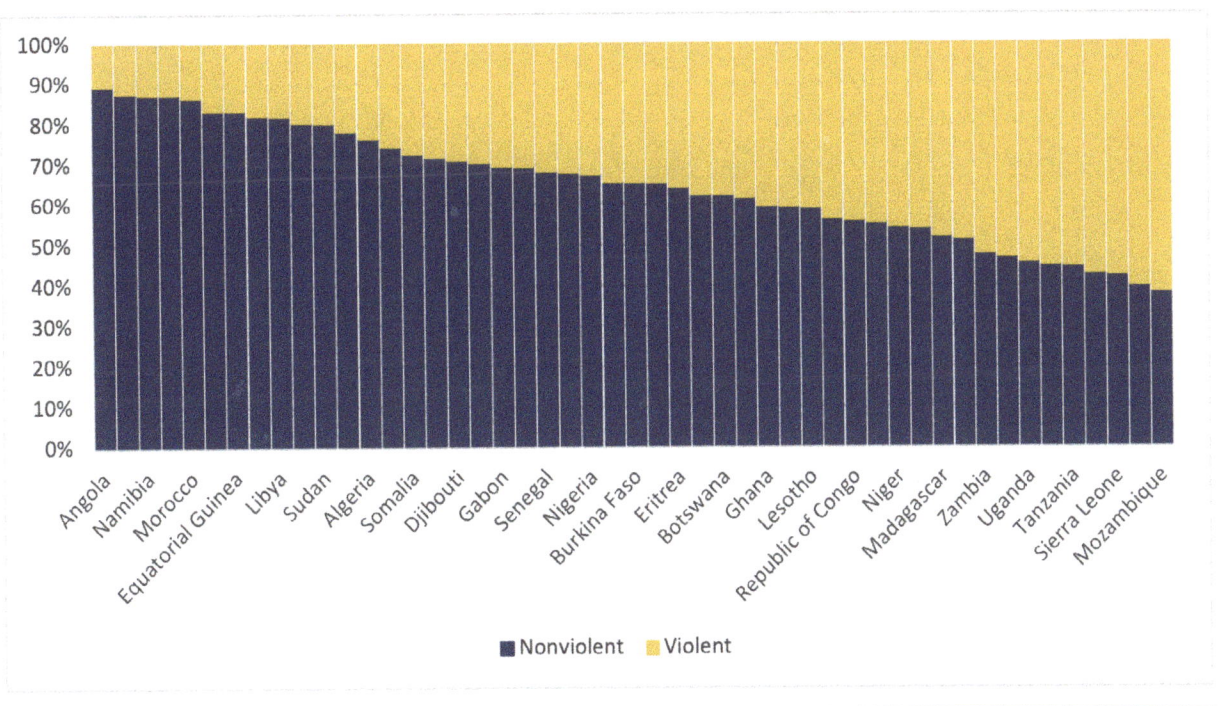

FIGURE 7. Proportion of Antigovernment Contention That Is Violent and Nonviolent

variation across regions in factors that may shape whether protests remain nonviolent or escalate into violent action, such as the presence and availability of police forces capable of repressing dissent, infrastructure such as roads that allow for coordinated tactical movement, and population density that may shape how many mobilize to protest. displays the proportion of contentious events in each country that were violent. Only contentious events that occurred during the years of Afrobarometer data collection (reflected in Table 5. Afrobarometer Rounds and Years) are included. In the left of the figure, countries like Angola, Rwanda, and Namibia experience very low levels of anti-government violent resistance incidents. In Angola, only 10.6 percent of all incidents are violent. On the right of the figure are those countries that experience a large proportion of violent events, including Sierra Leone, Malawi, and Mozambique. In Mozambique, 61.76 percent of all events are violent.

This initial visualization of nonviolent and violent conflict at the country level provides evidence that there are important state-level factors that shape nonviolent discipline within different countries. In order to incorporate these country-level effects, this study uses the approach of examining variation *within countries*. Thus, the relationship between trust and nonviolent action within subnational regions are analyzed. This approach has two distinct advantages. First, it allows for the analysis of a specific subnational region (defined as the first administrative district within a country[42]) over time. Thus, it is possible to test whether rising levels of social trust in Limpopo Province in South Africa lead to lower levels of violent anti-government action. This approach minimizes concerns about comparing trust and nonviolent action across different geographic regions, which may differ greatly from one another. Second, this allows for the comparison of different regions within the same country, which can reveal important information about how social trust may operate in some regions and not others. Within countries, there is often substantial variation across regions in factors that may shape whether protests remain nonviolent or escalate into violent action, such as the presence and availability of police forces capable of repressing dissent, infrastructure such as roads that allow for coordinated tactical movement, and population density that may shape how many mobilize to protest.

In each of the tests, higher social trust corresponds with higher proportions of contention that are nonviolent.

There are two major challenges that are worth noting before presenting the results of the tests. First, the Afrobarometer data are nationally representative but not subnationally representative. That is, while they provide a clear and accurate reflection of overall levels of social trust for each country in each year that the analysis was conducted, the same cannot be said about levels of social trust in each region of the country. This is certainly a challenge

---

42   First administrative districts correspond to the largest geographic region within a country. For example, in the United States, this would refer to the states themselves. In Switzerland, these are cantons.

because it means that the overall levels of social trust in, say, Lagos State in Nigeria may be different than the Afrobarometer data. This is a limitation of the data. As such, the results of the statistical test must be taken with some caution. Second, there is substantial variation from region to region in terms of the amount of contention one observes. Put simply, some regions experience more contention than others, and thus a region with a single violent riot experiences proportionally more violent action than a region with many contentious events, even if most of those events are themselves violent. This is inherent in the use of a proportional variable. Because this test is designed to roughly measure whether the individual-level preferences for nonviolent action correspond to less violent action, the measure holds; however, this approach constitutes simply a first step to measuring the relationship between trust and nonviolent discipline.

The majority of statistical information, including the output tables, are found in the statistical appendix. Because the output tested is the proportion of total conflict that was nonviolent, a linear regression model is used. The model is hierarchical, which means that it is programmed to nest each of the subnational regions within each country. This means that rather than simply comparing all regions against one another, it treats regions within countries differently than regions across different countries. In short, the model is able to better estimate the relationship between social trust and nonviolent discipline.

Next, the study runs a total of four models. The first model looks at the relationship between social trust ("most people can be trusted") and the proportion of conflict that is nonviolent. The second model uses measurements designed to test whether trust in a diverse population ("outgroup trust") complements the relationship between trust and nonviolent discipline. The third model uses a different measure of trust: trust in co-nationals. This is used because the first measurement of social trust is not asked in all rounds of the survey. Finally, the fourth model includes yet another form of trust: trust in acquaintances. These different forms of trust are included in order to trace, as thoroughly as possible, the relationship between many different forms of social trust and conflict.

In each model, the study also includes important factors that might shape whether conflict remains nonviolent or becomes violent. First, the study looks at overall evaluations of the present economy by residents of each given region. As discussed in Chapter 2, economic evaluations have long been considered important in the study of conflict. In Africa, this is particularly true; the Malian protests against former president Ibrahim Boubacar Kaïta that resulted in a coup in August 2020 were initiated by protesters seeking to reduce corruption and improve the economy. Second, the study looks at overall sentiments about the living conditions in each region. In South Africa, anger over low levels of public goods provision and high levels of poverty have generated a massive protest movement that the government has struggled to address (Alexander 2010; Booysen 2007; Chipkin 2013). Finally, the study includes a measurement of the overall level of employment in the region. Unemployed citizens are often able to devote substantial time and effort to joining civil resistance movements.

Results

The analysis provides mixed results.[43] In each of the tests, higher social trust corresponds with higher proportions of contention that are nonviolent. In the first model, while higher social trust does seem to correspond to higher levels of nonviolent action, the relationship is not statistically significant. In the second model, the relationship remains consistent—that is, higher social trust leads to more nonviolent action. In the third and fourth models, the different measurements of social trust do not significantly relate to more nonviolent action. This suggests that the predicted relationship is weak and highly contingent upon the inclusion of other factors in the analysis. At the same time, the consistency of the relationship between

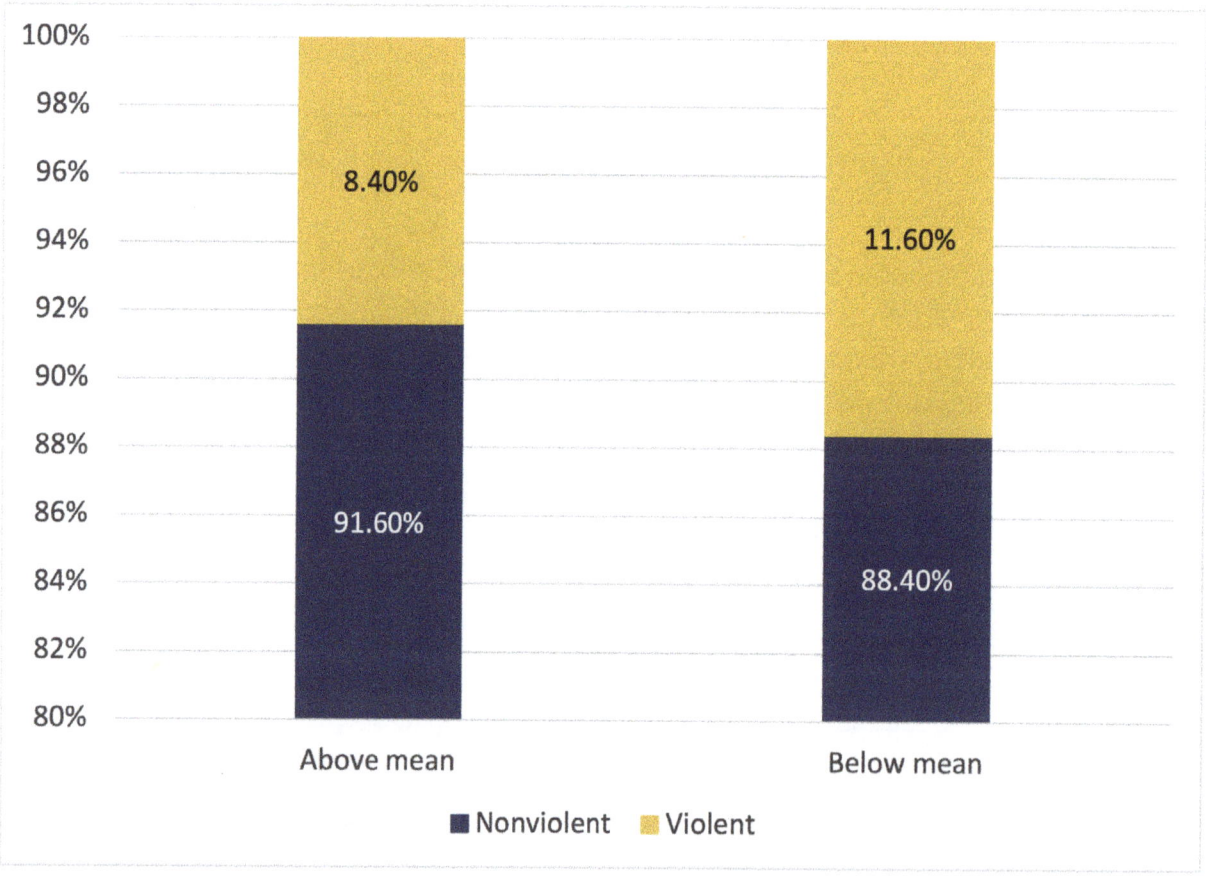

FIGURE 8. Generalized Trust and Predicted Antigovernment Nonviolent and Violent Actions

Note: Y-axis is limited to a window of 80 to 100 percent.

---

43 See Table 9 in the statistical appendix.

high levels of social trust and nonviolent action indicates that while the direct relationship may be weak, trust likely does play some role in maintaining nonviolent discipline.

Drawing from the second model, Figure 8. Generalized Trust and Predicted Antigovernment Nonviolent and Violent Actions presents the predicted effect of low or high trust on the proportion of conflict that is violent. The average level of social trust in an African region is 0.19, which indicates that 19 percent of respondents stated that "most people can be trusted."

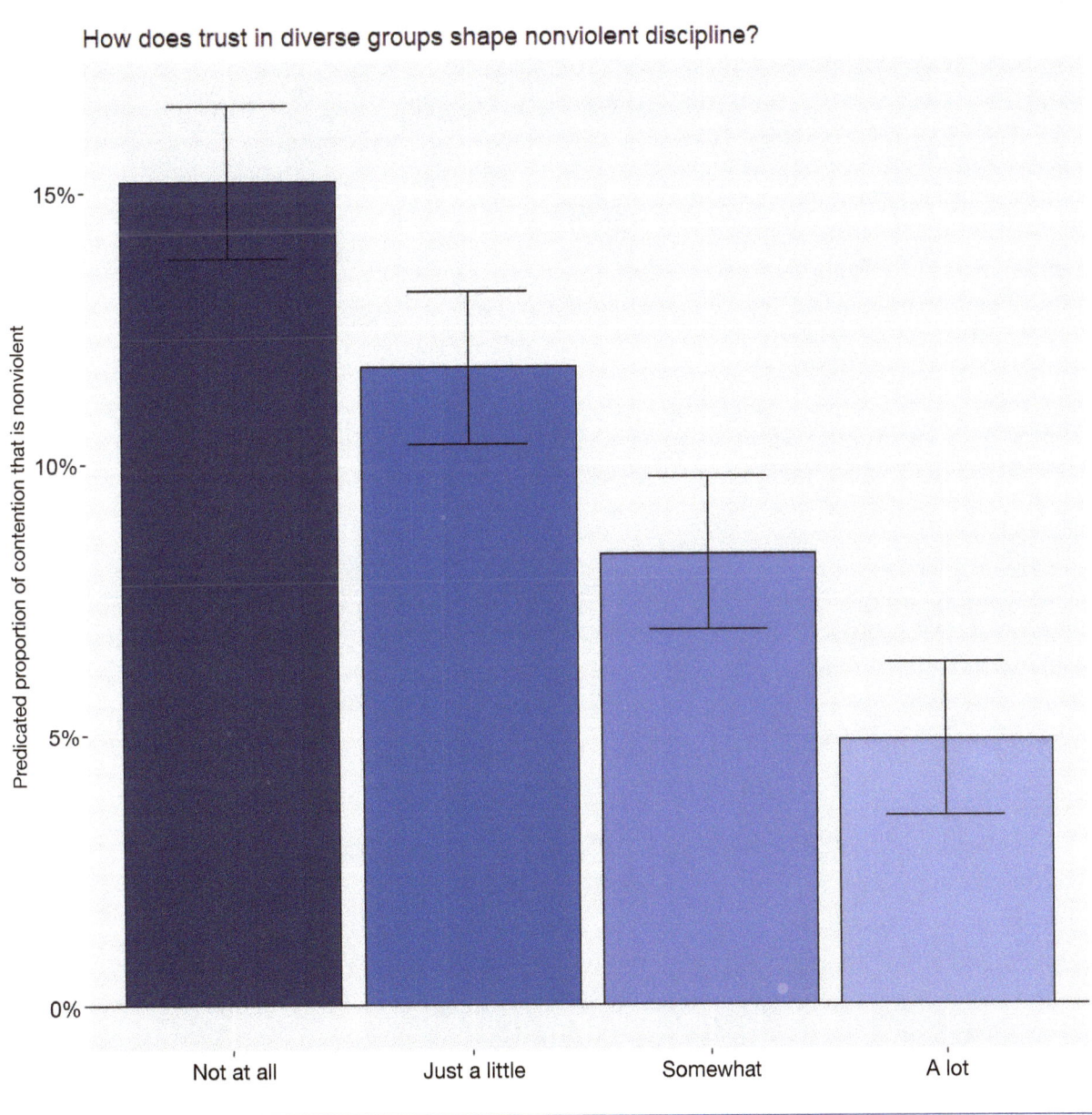

FIGURE 9. Trust in Diverse Groups and Predicted Nonviolent Contention

Thus, Figure 8. Generalized Trust and Predicted Antigovernment Nonviolent and Violent Actions presents the predicted proportion of total conflict that is violent for regions that fall below the mean ("lower levels of trust") and regions that fall above the mean ("higher levels of trust") in terms of average levels of social trust. For regions with lower levels of trust, approximately 11.6 percent of all conflict uses violent tactics. As trust increases, the predicted proportion of violence drops to 8.4 percent, comprising a 3.4 percentage point differential. This difference is rather small, though it is statistically significant.

The study now analyzes how trust in diverse populations and networks—that is, outgroup trust—shapes predicted levels of nonviolent discipline. Recall that because the outcome variable measures the proportion of conflict that is classified as violent, lower predictions are better. Holding all else equal, if a region was comprised entirely of individuals with no trust at all in diverse networks and populations, we would expect approximately 15 percent of all instances of conflict to include violent tactics. As trust in diverse populations and networks increases, the proportion of conflict that is violent drops dramatically. In a region in which the average amount of trust in diverse populations and networks is very high ("a lot"), we could expect that over 95 percent of conflicts would be conducted using nonviolent means and tactics.

Figure 9. Trust in Diverse Groups and Predicted Nonviolent Contention displays the relationship between trust in diverse groups and predicted levels of nonviolent contention. The x-axis represents four levels of how much respondents trust other co-nationals of different ethnicities, ranging from "not at all" on the left to "a lot" on the right. The y-axis represents the proportion of antigovernment contention that is violent. Thus, the smaller the bar, the lower the proportion of total contention that is violent. In regions where there are low levels of trust in diverse groups, over 15 percent of contentious events are violent. This drops sharply as trust in diverse groups increases. In regions where there is "a lot" of trust in diverse groups, the proportion of contention predicted to be violent is under 5 percent—a 67 percent reduction.

For civil resistance activists and scholars, this suggests that mobilizing broad, diverse networks of activists from across multiple ethnic groups is likely to improve nonviolent discipline. While the measurement used in this analysis captures ethnic diversity, other forms of diversity likely matter, including religious or linguistic diversity. The inclusion of broad and diverse coalitions is particularly important in Africa, where political power and access to goods are often distributed along ethnic lines. The anti-apartheid movement in the 1980s and 1990s in South Africa and the more recent anti-corruption movements in 2015 through 2018 drew upon broad coalitions of ethnic groups to oppose structural injustices (Laing 2015; Onishi 2017). Similarly, civil resistance movements in Egypt, Sudan, and Algeria drew from broad and diverse populations, all of which led to the overthrow of entrenched leaders and were primarily nonviolent. On the other hand, attempts by narrow, ethnically centered movements in Nigeria (Okonta and Douglas 2003; Onuoha 2012; Simpson 2014) and Kenya (Mariita 2018) have struggled to maintain nonviolent discipline in their campaigns for democracy and self-governance.

Summary of Chapter 3 Findings

This chapter has examined whether increased trust shapes nonviolent discipline via two methods. First, it used statistical analyses of whether Africans with high social trust voiced lower justification for the use of violent political action. It found very strong support for the prediction that high-trusting individuals prefer nonviolent action more than low-trusting individuals. Across each of the statistical tests, higher levels of trust correspond with an increased commitment to nonviolent action: high-trusting citizens stated very clearly that violence for political means is never justified. Each measurement of trust exhibited a statistically significant relationship.

In December 2018, following an increase in the price of bread, Sudanese citizens took to the streets to call for change.

Second, this chapter used statistical tests to measure whether aggregated levels of social trust correspond with higher proportions of nonviolent conflict. The tests provided mixed support for the prediction that regions with high reported levels of social trust experienced higher proportions of anti-state nonviolent action than regions with low levels of social trust. A total of six models were run. Across all models, social trust always corresponds with lower proportions of violent action. As in the previous chapter, this chapter tested multiple forms of trust, including generalized social trust ("most people can be trusted"), trust in co-nationals, and trust in acquaintances. In every model, these forms of social trust correspond with lower proportions of violent action. In two of the three models using generalized social trust, this relationship is statistically significant. Trust in co-nationals and trust in acquaintances were not found to have a significant relationship with whether the proportion of contention is violent or nonviolent.

In addition to measurements of social trust, measurements of trust in diverse groups (outgroup trust) at the individual-level were included, as was the observed proportions of conflict that were violent or nonviolent. At the individual level, high levels of trust in diverse populations corresponds with a reduced willingness to justify the use of violent actions. The results are strong and statistically significant.. When examining the observed proportions of conflict that are violent or nonviolent, the relationship remains consistent, though the result does not obtain statistical significance. It is unclear whether this is because the relationship does not hold up using observed data or whether the relatively small number of observations available to test this relationship impacted whether such a significant result could be found. Civil resistance movements have often focused on developing diverse networks of activists, and the African experience has often suggested that the more diverse a movement is, the more likely it is to maintain nonviolent discipline.

An excellent demonstration of this phenomenon can be found in the recent ouster of Sudan's 30-year dictator, Omar al-Bashir (Zunes 2021). In December 2018, following an increase in the price of bread, Sudanese citizens took to the streets to call for change. For many, these protests were long overdue; like many North African states, Sudan has long struggled to extend its economic development beyond the borders of Khartoum (Cockett 2016). For the Sudanese, the added economic burden of an increase in the price of bread proved to be the proverbial straw that broke the camel's back. From December 2018 through April 2019, a broad coalition of Sudanese citizens came together to demand the fall of Omar al-Bashir.

Similar to what happened in Tunisia and Egypt during the Arab Spring, there was no guarantee that these protests would remain nonviolent. Indeed, Omar al-Bashir's regime engaged directly in the repression of the protesters, seeking to remain in power. The International Crisis Group reported in early 2019 that the Sudanese forces, "accustomed to violent tactics, have shot into crowds and hurled teargas at protesters" (International Crisis Group 2019a, 4). Yet, despite the regime's use of an excessive level of repression, protesters generally remained peaceful. This nonviolent discipline has remained stalwart. Following the ouster of al-Bashir, the military took command of the country. Protesters stayed engaged, demanding a return to civilian rule (Wamsley 2019). On a number of occasions, the military opened fire upon protesters, killing and wounding many nonviolent civil resistance activists (Rashwan 2019b, 2019a; Van Sant and Matias 2019).

One factor that likely safeguarded against the use of violence by protesters was the broad nature of the protest coalition. As the International Crisis Group states, "Protesters come from mixed political and economic backgrounds. They include members of Sudan's longstanding leftist movements, the Sudanese Communist Party and the Sudanese Congress Party ... and a number of other political parties, along with professional trade unions, notably doctors, who are currently on strike" (International Crisis Group 2019a, 4). Indeed, what was striking—both before Bashir's ouster and after it—was the prominent role that women played in not only participating in, but leading, the protest movement (Bhalla 2019; Wedeman 2019). While these do not point specifically to the role that ethnicity did or did not play in the protests,[44] they do speak to the generally broad composition of the protests. Rather than

---

[44] There are pronounced ethnic divides within Sudan. For example, Omar al-Bashir's most trusted confidantes came from his ethnic group, the Riverine people (International Crisis Group 2019a).

developing ethnically or religiously oriented civil resistance demands, protesters developed a rather universal set of demands calling for civilian-led democratic rule—clearly shaped by the broad and diverse coalition that spearheaded the movement.

Resistance movements in other African countries have often struggled to organize around broad campaigns. For example, in countries where multiple powerful ethnic groups vie for power, anti-regime campaigns often take on ethnically or religiously oriented messaging. While these do not always result in violent movements, they often do. For example, following the defeat of Raila Odinga in the 2007 national election, ethnic riots devastated Kenya, leaving many dead and the political system greatly shaken (Human Rights Watch 2008; Ruteere 2011; Smith 2009).

Conclusion

What can this study tell us about the relationship between social trust and civil resistance? This monograph is comprised of two central predictions: that trust increases the willingness of Africans to engage in nonviolent protests and that trust improves the ability of civil resistance movements to maintain nonviolent discipline when challenging the government. Using statistical tests of survey data and observed conflict across the continent, this study tested these predictions and found that they are mostly supported, though additional research is merited. Table 6. Prediction Results presents these results with a short analysis.

Table 6. Prediction Results

PREDICTIONS	RESULT	STRENGTH OF EVIDENCE
Prediction 1: High levels of social trust correspond with an increased willingness to engage in nonviolent protests and demonstrations.	Mostly supported	Interpretation: Individuals that report high levels of social trust are more likely to express willingness to join a protest. Statistical results: Multiple regressions demonstrate positive and significant correlations, though not all measurements of trust obtain statistical significance. Relationships tested and correlations are robust to multiple specifications.
Prediction 2: High levels of social trust correspond with lower justifications for the use of violent action or observed violent action.	Partially supported	Interpretation: At the individual level, the more social trust that people have, the less likely they are to believe violence can be justified. This relationship is weaker when examining whether trust actually shapes whether conflict is violent or nonviolent. Statistical results: Multiple regressions produced varying outcomes. At the individual level, social trust corresponds to lower justification for violent action. Using observed data, multiple regressions demonstrated a weak and contingent relationship that only sometimes obtains significance.

Relevant Findings for Activists

A number of interesting lessons for nonviolent activists, organizations, and campaigns emerge out of the analysis. Understanding how to effectively capitalize on trust can be extremely challenging since it is difficult for a civil resistance organization to actively monitor or observe trust. With that said, this monograph suggests several potential avenues for mobilizing individuals into nonviolent action.

Focus on high-trust networks. Because mobilizing participants requires human and financial resources, activists and civil resistance movements should invest their efforts into drawing participants from existing trust networks, such as unions, civics organizations, well-formed student groups, and religious communities. Pre-existing organizations are likely to have already developed strong bonds of trust between members (Putnam 2001) and oftentimes civil resistance movements in Africa have emerged out of these communities. For example, South Africa's trade unions and religious organizations played central roles in the struggle against apartheid, and, more recently, student networks and anti-corruption NGOs were able to help mobilize many ordinary citizens to rise up against corruption and state capture by President Zuma (Runciman, Nkuna, and Frassinelli 2017). Civil resistance organizations should double their efforts to reach out to all types of organizations.

Focus on fostering cultures of trust within civil resistance campaigns. This study has focused on measuring the importance of trust among individuals and has provided evidence that high-trusting individuals serve as excellent candidates for civil resistance activists. But mobilizing such activists is only the first step. Once members are mobilized, civil resistance campaigns—and their constituent organizations—should focus heavily on developing strong bonds of trust that not only emphasize trusting one another but also the connective tissues of trust to the rest of the country. Evidence from other scholarship has shown that trust can be fostered via clear, consistent accountability mechanisms (Stamidis et al. 2019) for group decision-making, as well as the fostering of continuous relationships between members of a group (Mpande et al. 2013). This is likely to increase member participation, reduce demobilization, and improve nonviolent discipline.

Fostering cultures of trust within campaigns may also involve explicit trust-building exercises in which different civil resistance organizations participate. This has the potential to build interpersonal trust between activists, to enhance trust between civil resistance organizations, and to strengthen social linkages across the campaign. Goal-oriented exercises could include the collaborative development of organizational and campaign norms or perhaps the development of cross-organizational community engagement (e.g., campaigns providing support to their communities by providing foodstuffs or legal aid). By increasing the non-contentious interactions of civil resistance activists (within and between civil resistance organizations), campaigns can generate both rationalist trust expectations about the behavior of others within the campaign and broaden their moral community.

Civil resistance organizations should focus on developing broad campaigns rather than narrow, ethnic campaigns. The evidence suggests that trust in diverse populations and networks has a positive effect on maintaining nonviolent discipline. The statistical tests show that individuals that reported high levels of trust in diverse populations are significantly less likely to express justification for violent action. This finding is supported by evidence from recent diverse civil resistance campaigns in South Africa (Laing 2015), Tunisia (Bramsen 2018), and Algeria (Africa Research Bulletin 2019). Based on this finding, organizations that recruit and engage individuals with high levels of trust in diverse populations may improve campaign preferences for nonviolent action. One starting point may be to incorporate trade unions into civil resistance campaigns. Unions have a robust history in civil resistance across Africa (Bartkowski 2013; Bond and Mottiar 2013; Marinovich 2016), and an analysis of the Afrobarometer data indicates that members of trade unions have significantly higher levels of trust in diverse populations than non-union members.[45]

Of course, there are potential challenges. Building broad coalitions of diverse populations will require targeted—and often difficult—outreach to religious communities, ethnic communal organizations, and other similar groups in order to identify a common cause and to build trust between parties that might not otherwise work with one another. Work by Mueller (2018) and evidence from South Africa (Basson and Du Toit 2017; Booysen 2016; Laing 2015) indicate that civil resistance messages framed around economic underdevelopment may attract broad support. Still, there may be concerns that bringing together diverse populations could produce campaign in-fighting. Leaders of civil resistance organizations must coordinate together within the context of a larger campaign, and the products of that coordination should be communicated clearly and directly to their respective organizations. There is reason to be hopeful: the recent civil resistance movements in Sudan and Mali demonstrate that broad and diverse coalitions can successfully challenge entrenched, corrupt leaders.

Relevant Findings for Scholars

For scholars interested in civil resistance or the political psychology of conflict, this monograph has laid a foundation for future research and made several important findings. First, this research demonstrates a statistical relationship between high levels of social trust (measured through multiple variables) and several key factors that shape the emergence and success of civil resistance movements. A large body of scholarship has focused on individual-level mobilization in civil resistance, contentious politics, and conflict more broadly (Corrigall-Brown 2011; Kitschelt 1986; Viterna 2006, 2013; Wood 2003), and scholars of social trust have remarked on its effects on the potential for collective action (Benson and Rochon 2004; Habyarimana et al. 2009; Sønderskov 2011b). Yet the overall body of scholarship on trust as a central factor in mobilization remains small. This monograph contributes to this corpus by demonstrating that trust is a factor that should be incorporated more thoroughly into future research.

For scholars interested in the role that trust plays in shaping civil resistance—as well as conflict more broadly—this monograph reveals several potential avenues of future research.

---

45   See Table 10 in the appendix for the bivariate hierarchical regression results that support this.

Causality remains untested in this monograph, and experimental field research could shed light on how and why trust seems to motivate potential mobilization and increase preferences for nonviolent resistance. Several questions merit consideration. Do high levels of social trust motivate mobilization because high-trusting individuals believe in the trustworthiness of others, or are high-trusters instead motivated to produce public goods that can be shared broadly? How exactly do high-trusting individuals delineate their moral communities, and how does this differ from existing ethnic or religious communities?

Additionally, while this monograph made frequent references to civil resistance campaigns, it did not directly study the effects of trust on important factors like campaign cohesion, the ability of civil resistance organizations to coordinate with one another, the ability of civil resistance campaigns to bargain with the government, or the ability to restrain violent flanks. These factors are difficult to test, but extensive field research could provide important inroads into testing levels of trust between leaders of different civil resistance organizations within the same campaign.

A second contribution is the statistical testing of whether survey level data correspond to actual, observed political phenomena. This was tested twice. Chapter 3 looked at overall levels of nonviolent protest across Africa to gauge whether potential mobilization correlates with actual mobilization. The results suggest that they do, though further testing is required and will likely mandate field research. This contribution builds on a literature that has questioned the validity and reliability of responses given in surveys (Andersson and Granberg 1997) and suggests support for the finding that there is at least a weak correlation between expressed intent to support a cause and actual willingness to do so (Sweetman et al. 2019).

Third, this research expands the study of civil resistance to Africa, which is long overdue (Chabot and Vinthagen 2015). Africa has a rich history of civil resistance against corrupt and often brutal leaders, but it has been understudied. This is somewhat puzzling, given the frequency of civil resistance campaigns—large and small—across the continent. Africa's independence came in no small part due to sustained civil resistance campaigns that called for an end to colonization while the transition to multi-party democracy in the 1990s featured many nonviolent resistance movements standing strong against repressive leaders. Scholarly work in the 1990s did illustrate different paths of resistance against corrupt regimes (Bratton and van de Walle 1994), though the language of civil resistance was absent from the article. In recent years, other work has more successfully engaged African civil resistance and struggle (Bartkowski 2013; Naimark-Rowse 2017; Zeilig 2002). Future research should highlight African contributions to civil resistance further.

References

Africa Research Bulletin. "Black Bloc Militants: Amid Reports of Police Brutality and a State of Emergency in Three States, Protest against Mursi's Regime Continues." *Africa Research Bulletin* 50, no. 2 (2013): 19600–601.

———. "ALGERIA: Continuing Protests." *Africa Research Bulletin: Political, Social and Cultural Series* 56, no. 3 (2019): 22211A–22213C.

———. "MALI – Entrenched Opposition." *Africa Research Bulletin* 57, no. 7 (2020a): 22798B–22799B.

———. "ZIMBABWE: Crackdown Intensifies." *Africa Research Bulletin: Political, Social and Cultural Series* 57, no. 7 (2020b): 22813–15.

Afrobarometer. "Rounds 1–7, 1999–2018" (2019). **www.afrobarometer.org**.

Alexander, Peter. "Rebellion of the Poor: South Africa's Service Delivery Protests - a Preliminary Analysis." *Review of African Political Economy* 37, no. 123 (2010): 25–40.

Andersson, Hans E., and Donald Granberg. "On the Validity and Reliability of Self-Reported Vote: Validity Without Reliability?" *Quality & Quantity* 31 (1997): 127–40.

Ansolabehere, Stephen, and Eitan Hersh. "Validation: What Big Data Reveal About Survey Misreporting and the Real Electorate." *Political Analysis* 20 (2012): 437–59.

Auyero, Javier. "Relational Riot: Austerity and Corruption Protest in the Neoliberal Era." *Social Movement Studies* 2, no. 2 (2003): 117–145.

Axelrod, Robert. *The Evolution of Cooperation*. New York, NY: Basic Books, 2006.

Aytac, S. Erdem, and Susan C. Stoke. *Why Bother? Rethinking Participation in Elections and Protests*. New York, NY: Cambridge University Press, 2019.

Bartkowski, Maciej J. *Recovering Nonviolent History: Civil Resistance in Liberation Struggles*. Boulder, CO: Lynne Rienner Publishers, 2013. **https://www.nonviolent-conflict.org/wp-content/uploads/2018/08/Recovering-Nonviolent-History-Full-Text.pdf**.

Basson, Adriaan, and Pieter Du Toit. *Enemy of the People*. Jeppestown, SA: Jonathan Ball Publishers, 2017.

Beber, Bernd, Philip G. Roessler, and Alexandra Scacco. "Intergroup Violence and Political Attitudes: Evidence from a Dividing Sudan." *The Journal of Politics* 76, no. 03 (2014): 649–65. **http://dx.doi.org/10.1017/S0022381614000103**.

Benson, Michelle, and Thomas R. Rochon. "Interpersonal Trust and the Magnitude of Protest: A Micro and Macro Level Approach." *Comparative Political Studies* 37, no. 4 (2004): 435–57.

Beyerle, Shaazka. *Curtailing Corruption: People Power for Accountability and Justice*. Boulder, CO: Lynne Rienner Publishers, 2014.

Bhalla, Nita. "'The Revolution Isn't over' Say Sudan's Frontline Female Protesters." *Reuters*. September 19, 2019. **https://news.trust.org/item/20190919223445-gji9u/**.

Bond, Patrick, and Shauna Mottiar. "Movements, Protests and a Massacre in South Africa." *Journal of Contemporary African Studies* 31, no. 2 (2013): 283–302.

Booth, Jeb A., Amy Farrell, and Sean P. Varano. "Social Control, Serious Delinquency, and Risky Behavior: A Gendered Analysis." *Crime & Delinquency* 54, no. 3 (2008): 423–456.

Booysen, Susan. "With the Ballot and the Brick: The Politics of Attaining Service Delivery." *Progress in Development Studies* 7 no. 1 (2007): 21–32.

———. *Dominance and Decline: The ANC in the Time of Zuma*. Johannesburg, SA: Wits University Press, 2015.

———. "Introduction." In *Fees Must Fall: Student Revolt, Decolonization, and Governance in South Africa*, edited by Susan Booysen. Johannesburg, SA: Wits University Press, 2016.

Bramsen, Isabel. "How Civil Resistance Succeeds (or Not): Micro-Dynamics of Unity, Timing, and Escalatory Actions." *Peace & Change* 43, no. 1 (2018): 61–89.

———. "Avoiding Violence: Eleven Ways Activists Can Confine Violence in Civil Resistance Campaigns." *Conflict Resolution Quarterly* 36, no. 4 (2019): 329–44.

Branch, Adam, and Zachariah Cherian Mampilly. *Africa Uprising: Popular Protest and Political Change*. London, England: Zed Books, 2015.

Bratton, Michael, and Nicolas van de Walle. "Neopatrimonial Regimes and Political Transitions in Africa Michael Bratton." *World Politics* 46, no. 4 (1994): 453–89.

———. *Democratic Experiments in Africa: Regime Transitions in Comparative Perspective*. New York, NY: Cambridge University Press, 1997.

Buchanan, Larry, Quoctrung Bui, and Jugal K. Patel. "Black Lives Matter May Be the Largest Movement in U.S. History." *The New York Times*. July 3, 2020. **https://www.nytimes.com/interactive/2020/07/03/us/george-floyd-protests-crowd-size.html**.

Butcher, Charles, and Isak Svensson. "Manufacturing Dissent: Modernization and the Onset of Major Nonviolent Resistance Campaigns." *Journal of Conflict Resolution* 60, no. 2 (2016): 311–39.

Caillier, James. "Citizen Trust, Political Corruption, and Voting Behavior: Connecting the Dots." *Politics and Policy* 38, no. 5 (2010): 1015–35.

Cederman, Lars-Erik, Nils B. Weidmann, and Kristian Skrede Gleditsch. "Horizontal Inequalities and Ethnonationalist Civil War: A Global Comparison." *American Political Science Review* 105, no. 3 (2011): 478–95. **http://www.journals.cambridge.org/abstract_S0003055411000207**.

Chabot, Sean, and Stellan Vinthagen. "Decolonizing Civil Resistance." *Mobilization* 20, no. 4 (2015): 517–32.

Chaurand, Nadine, and Markus Brauer. "What Determines Social Control? People's Reactions to Counternormative Behaviors in Urban Environments." *Journal of Applied Social Psychology* 38, no. 7(2008): 1689–1715.

Chenoweth, Erica. *The Success of Nonviolent Civil Resistance*. Filmed November 2013 at TEDxBoulder, Boulder, CO. Video, 12:33. **https://tedxboulder.com/speakers/erica-chenoweth**.

Chenoweth, Erica, and Kurt Schock. "Do Contemporaneous Armed Challenges Affect the Outcomes of Mass Nonviolent Campaigns?" *Mobilization* 20, no. 4 (2015): 427–51.

Chenoweth, Erica, and Maria J. Stephan. *Why Civil Resistance Works: The Strategic Logic of Nonviolent Conflict*. New York, NY: Columbia University Press, 2011.

Chenoweth, Erica, and Jay Ulfelder. "Can Structural Conditions Explain the Onset of Nonviolent Uprisings?" *Journal of Conflict Resolution* 61, no. 2 (2017): 298–324.

Chipkin, Ivor. "Whither the State ? Corruption , Institutions and State-Building in South Africa." *Politikon* 40, no. 2 (2013): 211–31.

Chong, Dennis. *Collective Action and the Civil Rights Movement*. Chicago, IL: University of Chicago Press, 1991.

Cockett, Richard. *Sudan: Darfur and the Failure of an African State, 2nd edition*. New Haven, CT: Yale University Press, 2016.

Collins, Randall. *Violence: A Micro-Sociological Theory*. Princeton, NJ: Princeton University Press, 2008.

Cook, Karen S., Russell Hardin, and Margaret Levi. *Cooperation Without Trust?* New York, NY: Russell Sage Foundation, 2005.

Corrigall-Brown, Catherine. *Patterns of Protest: Trajectories of Participation in Social Movements*. Stanford, CA: Stanford University Press, 2011.

Crepaz, Markus M.L., Karen Bodnaruk Jazayeri, and Jonathan Polk. "What's Trust Got to Do With It? The Effects of In-Group and Out-Group Trust on Conventional and Unconventional Political Participation." *Social Science Quarterly* 98, no. 1 (2017): 261–81.

Dahlum, Sirianne, and Tore Wig. "Chaos on Campus: Universities and Mass Political Protest." *Comparative Political Studies* (2020).

Daxecker, Ursula E., and Michael L. Hess. "Repression Hurts: Coercive Government Responses and the Demise of Terrorist Campaigns." *British Journal of Political Science* 43, no. 3 (2013): 559–77.

Dudouet, Veronique. *Civil Resistance and Conflict Transformation: Transitions from Armed to Nonviolent Struggle*. New York, NY: Routledge, 2015.

Dudouet, Véronique. "Dynamics and Factors of Transition from Armed Struggle to Nonviolent Resistance." *Journal of Peace Research* 50, no. 3 (2013): 401–13.

Ensminger, Jean. "Reputations, Trust, and the Principal Agent Problem." In *Trust in Society*, edited by Karen S. Cook. New York, NY: Russell Sage Foundation, 2001.

Evelyne Musambi. "Kenyans to Take Mega Corruption Protest to the Streets - Nairobi News." *Nairobi News*. May 26, 2018. **https://nairobinews.nation.co.ke/news/kenyans-protests-corruption-streets/**.

Fujii, Lee Ann. "The Power of Local Ties: Popular Participation in the Rwandan Genocide." *Security Studies* 17, no. 3 (2008): 568–97.

Glaeser, Stephanie. "The Irony of Social Trust: Individual-Level and Contextual-Level Links with Protest Intention and Radical Right Support in Switzerland." *Journal of Community & Applied Social Psychology* 26 (2016): 110–24.

Godwin, Peter. *The Fear: Robert Mugabe and the Martyrdom of Zimbabwe*. New York, NY: Back Bay Books, 2011.

Gould, Roger V. "Multiple Networks and Mobilization in the Paris Commune, 1871." *American Sociological Review* 56 (1991): 716–29.

———. "Collective Action and Network Structure." *American Sociological Review* 58, no. 2 (1993): 182.

———. *Insurgent Identities: Class, Co Mmunity, and Protest in Paris from 1948 to the Commune*. Chicago, IL: University of Chicago Press, 1995.

Graham-Harrison, Emma. "'No Exams Until Mugabe Resigns': Zimbabwe Students in Mass Boycott." *The Guardian*. November 20, 2017. **https://www.theguardian.com/world/2017/nov/20/no-exams-until-mugabe-resigns-zimbabwe-students-mass-boycott**.

Granovetter, Mark S. "The Strength of Weak Ties." *American Journal of Sociology* 78, no. 6 (1973): 1360–80.

Gregg, Richard. *The Power of Nonviolence.* 8th edition. New York, NY: Cambridge University Press, 2018.

Gurr, Ted Robert. *Why Men Rebel.* 40th Anniv. Boulder, CO: Paradigm Publishers, 1970.

Habyarimana, James, Macartan Humphreys, Daniel N. Posner, and Jeremy M. Weinstein. *Coethnicity: Diversity and Dilemmas of Collective Action.* New York, NY: Russell Sage Foundation, 2009.

Hari, Solomon Ibrahim. "The Evolution of Social Protest in Nigeria: The Role of Social Media in the '#OccupyNigeria' Protest." *International Journal of Humanities and Social Science Invention* 3, no. 9 (2014): 2319–7714.

Hirschi, Travis. *Causes of Delinquency.* Berkeley, CA: University of California Press, 1969.

Human Rights Watch. "Ballots to Bullets: Organized Political Violence and Kenya's Crisis of Governance." *Human Rights Watch.* March 16, 2008. https://www.hrw.org/report/2008/03/16/ballots-bullets/organized-political-violence-and-kenyas-crisis-governance.

Hussein, Ebtisam. "The 2019 Algerian Protests: A Belated Spring?" *Middle East Policy* 26, no. 4 (2019): 131–45.

Ihonvbere, Julius O. "Where Is the Third Wave? A Critical Evaluation of Africa's Non-Transition to Democracy." *Africa Today* 43, no. 4 (1996).

International Crisis Group. *Improving Prospects for Peaceful Transition in Sudan.* January 14, 2019a. https://www.crisisgroup.org/africa/horn-africa/sudan/b143-improving-prospects-peaceful-transition-sudan.

———. *Safeguarding Sudan's Revolution.* October 21, 2019b. https://www.crisisgroup.org/africa/horn-africa/sudan/281-safeguarding-sudans-revolution.

Ives, Brandon J., and Jacob S. Lewis. "From Rallies to Riots: Why Some Protests Become Violent." *Journal of Conflict Resolution* 64, no. 5 (2020): 958–986.

Johnston, Michael. *Civil Society and Corruption: Mobilizing for Reform.* Lanham, MD: University Press of America, 2005.

Kitschelt, Herbert P. "Political Opportunity Structures and Political Protest: Anti-Nuclear Movements in Four Democracies." *British Journal of Political Science* 16, no. 1 (1986): 57–85.

Laing, Aislinn. "'Zuma Must Fall' Rallies against South African President Across the Country." *The Telegraph.* December 16, 2015. https://www.telegraph.co.uk/news/worldnews/africaandindianocean/southafrica/12053485/Zuma-Must-Fall-rallies-against-South-African-president-across-the-country.html.

Lancaster, Lizette. "Unpacking Discontent: Where and Why Protest Happens in South Africa." *South African Crime Quarterly* 64 (2018): 29–44.

Larmer, Miles. "Resisting the State: The Trade Union Movement and Working-Class Politics in Zambia, 1964–91." In *Class Struggle and Resistance in Africa*, edited by Leo Zeilig. Chicago, IL: Haymarket Books, 2009. 157–77.

LeBas, Adrienne. *From Protest to Parties: Party-Building & Democratization in Africa.* New York, NY: Oxford University Press, 2011.

Lee, Aie-Rie, and Yong U. Glasure. "Social Capital and Political Participation in South Korea." *Asian Affairs: An American Review* 34, no. 2 (2007): 101–18.

Levi, Margaret. "A State of Trust." In *Trust & Governance*, edited by Valerie Braithwaite and Margaret Levi. New York, NY: Russell Sage Foundation, 1998. 77–101.

Lewis, Jacob S. "Corruption Perceptions and Contentious Politics in Africa: How Different Types of Corruption Have Shaped Africa's Third Wave of Protest." *Political Studies Review* (2020): 1–18.

Lichbach, Mark I. *The Rebel's Dilemma*. Ann Arbor, MI: University of Michigan Press, 1995.

Lubell, Mark. "Familiarity Breeds Trust: Collective Action in a Policy Domain." *The Journal of Politics* 69, no. 1 (2007): 237–50.

Mackie, Diane M., and Mi Na Ahn. "Ingroup and Outgroup Inferences: When Ingroup Bias Overwhelms Outcome Bias." *European Journal of Social Psychology* 28, no. 3 (1998): 343–60.

Madonsela, Thuli. *State of Capture*. Johannesburg, SA: Public Protector, 2016.

Mampilly, Zachariah Cherian. *Rebel Rulers: Insurgent Governance and Civilian Life During War*. Ithaca, NY: Cornell University Press, 2011.

Mariita, Abraham. "#STOPtheseThieves – Demo Against Corruption – Action for Transparency." *Action for Transparency* (2018). https://actionfortransparency.org/stopthesethieves-demo-against-corruption/ (Accessed February 19, 2019).

Marinovich, Greg. *Murder at Small Koppie: The Real Story of the Marikana Massacre*. Ann Arbor, MI: Michigan State University Press, 2016.

Martin, Brian. "From Political Jiu-Jitsu to the Backfire Dynamic: How Repression Can Promote Mobilization." In *Civil Resistance: Comparative Perspectives on Nonviolent Struggle*, edited by Kurt Schock. Minneapolis, MN: University of Minnesota Press, 2015. *145–67*. https://www.bmartin.cc/pubs/15Schock.html.

Marwell, Gerald, E. Oliver, Pamela, and Ralph Prahl. "Social Networks and Collective Action: A Theory of the Critical Mass." *American Journal of Sociology* 94, no. 3 (1988): 502–34.

McAdam, Doug. "Recruitment to High-Risk Activism: The Case of Freedom Summer." *American Journal of Sociology* 92, no. 1 (1986): 64–90.

McClendon, Gwyneth, and Rachel Beatty Riedl. "Religion as a Stimulant of Political Participation: Experimental Evidence from Nairobi, Kenya." *Journal of Politics* 77, no. 4 (2015): 1045–57.

Mendilow, Jonathan, and Ilan Peleg. *Corruption and Government Legitimacy*. Washington, DC: Lexington Books, 2016.

Momba, Jotham C., and Fay Gadsden. "Zambia: Nonviolent Strategies Against Colonialism." In *Recovering Nonviolent History: Civil Resistance in Liberation Struggles*, edited by Maciej Bartkowski. Boulder, CO: Lynne Rienner Publishers, 2013. 71–88.

Mpande, Eugenia et al. "Community Intervention During Ongoing Political Violence: What Is Possible? What Works?" *Peace and Conflict* 19, no. 2 (2013): 196–208.

Mueller, Lisa. "Democratic Revolutionaries or Pocketbook Protesters? The Roots of the 2009–2010 Uprisings in Niger." *African Affairs* 112, no. 448 (2013): 398–420.

———. *Political Protest in Contemporary Africa*. New York, NY: Cambridge University Press, 2018.

Naimark-Rowse, Benjamin R. "Surviving Success: Nonviolent Rebellion in Sudan." *Journal of Peacebuilding and Development* 12, no. 3 (2017): 117–23.

New York Amsterdam News. "Anti-Apartheid 'Black Sash' Activist Passes." *New York Amsterdam News*, 2010.

Nilson, Douglas C., and Linda Burzotta Nilson. "Trust in Elites and Protest Orientation: An Integrative Approach." *Political Behavior* 2, no. 4 (1980): 385–404.

Nordas, Ragnhild, and Christian A. Davenport. "Fight the Youth: Youth Bulges and State Repression." *American Journal of Political Science* 57, no. 4 (2013): 926–40.

North, Douglass C. "Transaction Costs, Institutions, and Economic History." *Journal of Institutional and Theoretical Economics* 140 (1984): 7–17.

———. "Institutions." *Journal of Economic Perspectives* 5, no. 1 (1991): 97–112.

Nyadu, Anathi, and Thabo Twala. "#FeesMustFall: Tension, Violence in Second Week of #UFSShutdown." *IOL*. October 26, 2017. **https://www.iol.co.za/news/south-africa/feesmustfall-tension-violence-in-second-week-of-ufsshutdown-11716570** (Acceesed July 16, 2019).

O'Donnell, JefCoate, and Robbie Gramer. "Cameroon's Paul Biya Gives a Master Class in Fake Democracy." *Foreign Policy*. October 22, 2018. **https://foreignpolicy.com/2018/10/22/cameroons-paul-biya-gives-a-master-class-in-fake-democracy/** (Accessed April 11, 2019).

Okonta, Ike, and Oronto Douglas. *Where Vultures Feast: Shell, Human Rights, and Oil*. London, England: Verso, 2003.

Olson, Mancur. *The Logic of Collective Action*. Cambridge, MA: Harvard University Press, 1965.

Onishi, Normitsu. "Thousands March in South Africa to Demand Jacob Zuma's Resignation." *New York Times*. April 7, 2017. **https://www.nytimes.com/2017/04/07/world/africa/south-africa-jacob-zuma-protests.html** (Accessed September 16, 2017).

Onuoha, Godwin. "Contemporary Igbo Nationalism and the Crisis of Self-Determination in Nigeria." *African Studies* 71, no. 1 (2012): 29–51.

Osha, Sanya. "Birth of the Ogoni Protest Movement." *Journal of Asian and African Studies* 41, nos. 1–2 (2006): 13–38. **http://jas.sagepub.com/cgi/doi/10.1177/0021909606061746**.

Østby, Gudrun. "Polarization, Horizontal Inequalities and Violent Civil Conflict." *Journal of Peace Research* 45, no. 2 (2008): 143–62.

Pinckney, Jonathan. *Making or Breaking Nonviolent Discipline in Civil Resistance Movements*. Washington, DC: ICNC Press, 2016. **https://www.nonviolent-conflict.org/resource/making-breaking-nonviolent-discipline-civil-resistance-movements/**.

———. *When Civil Resistance Succeeds Building Democracy After Popular Nonviolent Uprisings*. Washington, DC: ICNC Press. **https://www.nonviolent-conflict.org/resource/civil-resistance-succeeds-building-democracy-popular-nonviolent-uprisings/**.

Presbey, Gail. "Ghana: Nonviolent Resistance in the Independence Movement, 1890s-1950s." In *Recovering Nonviolent History: Civil Resistance in Liberation Struggles*, edited by Maciej Bartkowski. Boulder, CO: Lynne Rienner Publishers, 2013. 51–70.

Putnam, Robert. *Bowling Alone: The Collapse and Revival of American Community*. New York, NY: Simon & Schuster, 2001.

Raden, David. "Ingroup Bias, Classic Ethnocentrism, and Non-Ethnocentrism Among American Whites." *Political Psychology* 24, no. 4 (2003): 803–28.

Raleigh, Clionadh, Andrew Linke, Håvard Hegre, and Joakim Karlsen. "Introducing ACLED: An Armed Conflict Location and Event Dataset: Special Data Feature." *Journal of Peace Research* 47, no. 5 (2010): 651–60.

Ramzy, Austin, and Mike Ives. "Hong Kong Protest, One Year Later." *New York Times.* June 9, 2020. **https://www.nytimes.com/2020/06/09/world/asia/hong-kong-protests-one-year-later.html**.

Rashwan, Nada. "Four Killed at Sudan Protest, and Tensions Rise." *The New York Times*. August 1, 2019a. **https://www.nytimes.com/2019/08/01/world/middleeast/sudan-protest-killed.html**.

———. "Killing of Student Protesters in Sudan Sets Off New Unrest, and Worry." *The New York Times*. July 30, 2019b. **https://www.nytimes.com/2019/07/30/world/africa/sudan-protest-killing.html**.

Rørbæk, Lasse Lykke. "Ethnic Exclusion and Civil Resistance Campaigns: Opting for Nonviolent or Violent Tactics?" *Terrorism and Political Violence* 31, no. 3 (2019): 475–93. **https://doi.org/10.1080/09546553.2016.1233872**.

Rotberg, Robert I. "Failed States, Collapsed States, Weak States: Causes and Indicators." In *State Failure and State Weakness In a Time of Terror,* edited by Robert I. Rotberg. Washington, DC: Brookings Institution, 2003. 1–26.

Runciman, Carin. "The 'Ballot and the Brick': Protest, Voting and Non-Voting in Post-Apartheid South Africa." *Journal of Contemporary African Studies* 34, no. 4 (2016): 419–36.

Runciman, Carin, Linah Nkuna, and Pier Paolo Frassinelli. "Survey Sheds Light on Who Marched Agains President Zuma and Why." *The Conversation*. April 20, 2017. **http://theconversation.com/survey-sheds-light-on-who-marched-against-president-zuma-and-why-76271** (Accessed January 23, 2020).

Ruteere, Mutuma. "More than Political Tools: The Police and Post-Election Violence in Kenya." *African Security Review* 20, no. 4 (2011): 11–20.

Ryckman, Kirssa Cline. "A Turn to Violence: The Escalation of Nonviolent Movements." *Journal of Conflict Resolution* 64, nos. 2–3 (2020): 318–43.

Van Sant, Shannon, and Dani Matias. "Sudanese Security Forces Open Fire On Protesters In Capital." *National Public Radio*. June 3, 2019. **https://www.npr.org/2019/06/03/729329601/sudan-security-forces-open-fire-on-protesters-in-capital**.

Schock, Kurt. "People Power and Political Opportunities: Social Movement Mobilization and Outcomes in the Philippines and Burma." *Social Problems* 46, no. 3 (1999): 355–75.

———. *Unarmed Insurrections: People Power Movements in Nondemocracies*. Minneapolis, MN: University of Minnesota Press, 2005.

———. "The Practice and Study of Civil Resistance." *Journal of Peace Research* 50, no. 3 (2013): 277–90.

Security, National. "SUDAN: Protests Grow." *Africa Research Bulletin: Political, Social and Cultural Series* 56, no. 2 (2019): 22202B–22204A.

Sharp, Gene. *The Politics of Nonviolent Action: I, II, & III*. Porter Sargent Publishers, 1973.

———. *How Nonviolent Struggle Works*. Boston, MA: Albert Einstein Institute, 2013. **www.aeinstein.org**.

Simpson, Brad. "The Biafran Secession and the Limits of Self-Determination." *Journal of Genocide Research* 16, nos. 2–3 (2014): 337–54. **http://dx.doi.org/10.1080/14623528.2014.936708**.

Sinwell, Luke, and Siphiwe Mbatha. *The Spirit of Marikana: The Rise of Insurgent Trade Unionism in South Africa*. London, UK: Pluto Press, 2016.

Smith, Lahra. "Explaining Violence after Recent Elections in Ethiopia and Kenya." *Democratization* 16, no. 5 (2009): 867–97.

Snow, David A., Louis A. Zurcher Jr., and Sheldon Ekland-Olson. "Social Networks and Social Movements: A Microstructural Approach to Differential Recruitment." *American Sociological Review* 45, no. 5 (1980): 787–801.

Sønderskov, Kim Mannemar. "Different Goods, Different Effects: Exploring the Effects of Generalized Social Trust in Large-N Collective Action." *Public Choice* 140, nos. 1–2 (2009): 145–60.

———. "Does Generalized Social Trust Lead to Associational Membership? Unravelling a Bowl of Well-Tossed Spaghetti." *European Sociological Review* 27, no. 4 (2011a): 419–34.

———. "Explaining Large-N Cooperation: Generalized Social Trust and the Social Exchange Heuristic." *Rationality and Society* 23, no. 1 (2011b): 51–74.

Sønderskov, Kim Mannemar, and Peter Thisted Dinesen. "Trusting the State, Trusting Each Other? The Effect of Institutional Trust on Social Trust." *Political Behavior* 38, no. 1 (2016): 179–202.

Stamidis, Katherine V. et al. "Trust, Communication, and Community Networks: How the Core Group Polio Project Community Volunteers Led the Fight against Polio in Ethiopia's Most at-Risk Areas." *American Journal of Tropical Medicine and Hygiene* 101, no. 4 (2019): 59–67.

Steenkamp, Jan Benedict E.M., Martijn G. De Jong, and Hans Baumgartner. "Socially Desirable Response Tendencies in Survey Research." *Journal of Marketing Research* 47, no. 2 (2010): 199–214.

van Stekelenburg, Jacquelien, and Bert Klandermans. "In Politics We Trust...or Not? Trusting and Distrusting Demonstrators Compared." *Political Psychology* 39, no. 4 (2018): 775–92.

Stewart, Frances. *Horizontal Inequalities and Conflict: Understanding Group Violence in Multiethnic Societies*. London, England: Palgrave MacMillan, 2010.

Sullivan, Heather. "Sticks, Stones, and Broken Bones: Protest Violence and the State." *Journal of Conflict Resolution* 63, no. 3 (2018): 1–27.

Sweetman, Joseph et al. "Attitude Toward Protest Uniquely Predicts (Normative and Nonnormative) Political Action by (Advantaged and Disadvantaged) Group Members." *Journal of Experimental Social Psychology* 82 (2019): 115–28. (Accessed November 2018). **https://doi.org/10.1016/j.jesp.2019.01.001**.

Tajfel, Henri, and John C. Turner. "The Social Identity Theory of Integroup Behavior." In *Psychology of Integroup Relations*, edited by Stephen Worchel and William G. Austin. Chicago, IL: Blackwell, 1986.

Thompson, Leonard. *A History of South Africa*. 4th edition. New Haven, CT: Yale University Press, 2014.

Thurber, Ches. "Social Ties and the Strategy of Civil Resistance." *International Studies Quarterly* 63, no. 4 (2019): 974–86.

Tilly, Charles. *Trust and Rule*. New York, NY: Cambridge University Press, 2005.

Tufekci, Zeynep. *Twitter and Tear Gas*. New Haven: Yale University Press, 2017.

Uslaner, Eric M. *The Moral Foundations of Trust*. New York, NY: Cambridge University Press, 2002.

———. *Corruption, Inequality, and the Rule of Law*. New York, NY: Cambridge University Press, 2008.

Viterna, Jocelyn S. "Pulled, Pushed, and Persuaded: Explaining Women's Mobilization into the Salvadoran Guerrilla Army." *American Journal of Sociology* 112, no. 1 (2006): 1–45.

———. *Women in War: The Micro-Processes of Mobilization in El Salvador.* New York, NY: Oxford University Press, 2013.

Wamsley, Laurel. "Pro-Democracy Protests Fill Streets In Sudan, Calling For Civilian Control." *National Public Radio.* July 1, 2019. **https://www.npr.org/2019/07/01/737638806/pro-democracy-protests-fill-streets-in-sudan-calling-for-civilian-control**.

Wedeman, Ben. "Activists Were Killed and Women Were Raped. But Some Defiant Sudanese Say Their Revolution Isn't Over Yet." *CNN.* June 6, 2019. **https://www.cnn.com/2019/06/20/africa/sudan-crackdown-rsf-wedeman-intl/index.html**.

Wickham-Crowley, Timothy P. *Guerrillas and Revolution in Latin America: A Comparative Study of Insurgents and Regimes Since 1956.* Princeton, NJ: Princeton University Press, 1992.

Wood, Elisabeth Jean. *Insurgent Collective Action and Civil War in El Salvador.* New York, NY: Cambridge University Press, 2003.

Zeilig, Leo. *Class Struggle and Resistance in Africa.* Chicago, IL: Haymarket Books, 2002.

Zunes, Stephen. *Civil Resistance Against Coups: A Comparative and Historical Perspective.* Washington, DC: ICNC Press, 2017. **https://www.nonviolent-conflict.org/resource/civil-resistance-coups-comparative-historical-perspective/**.

———. *Sudan's 2019 Revolution: The Power of Civil Resistance.* Washington, DC: ICNC Press, 2021. **https://www.nonviolent-conflict.org/resource/sudans-2019-revolution-the-power-of-civil-resistance/**.

Statistical Appendix

Overview

In this appendix, I provide the unstandardized coefficient results from the models tested in each chapter. For scholars and statistically adept activists, this appendix will provide important insight into the nuance, strengths, and limitations of the models that were run and reported on in the main text. For those seeking to replicate the statistics in this monograph, the statistical script and data can be requested by emailing the author at **js.lewis@wsu.edu**.

Statistical Information from Chapter 2

In Chapter 2, the first test examines whether different forms of trust shape a self-reported willingness to mobilize, which I refer to as potential mobilization. The independent variables are different forms of trust (generalized social trust, trust in co-nationals, trust in neighbors, and trust in acquaintances). Below, I present descriptive information about these variables. Note that the variable for generalized trust is dichotomous.

Table 7. Descriptive Statistics for Trust Variables

TYPE OF TRUST	MIN.	1ST QUART.	MEDIAN	MEAN	3RD QUART.	MAX
Generalized social trust	0.00	0.00	0.00	0.18	0.00	1.00
Trust in co-nationals	0.00	1.00	1.00	1.33	2.00	3.00
Trust in neighbors	0.00	1.00	2.00	1.76	3.00	3.00
Trust in acquaintances	0.00	1.00	1.00	1.46	2.00	3.00

Table 7 includes the primary results from Chapter 2. The dependent variable is potential mobilization, and the model is a hierarchical (multilevel) ordinary least squares regression with random slopes and intercepts structured at the country level. In three of the four models, 33 countries are tested. In Model 3, only 20 countries are tested. This is a limitation of the round of data that included the question about trust in co-nationals.

Table 8 displays the unstandardized coefficients for the results of the first statistical finding in this chapter. The model is a hierarchical ordinary least squares regression with random slopes and intercepts structured at the country level.

Table 8. Linear Regression of Potential Mobilization with Full Sample

	MODEL 1	MODEL 2	MODEL 3	MODEL 4
Intercept	0.394***	0.391***	0.591***	0.417***
	(0.042)	(0.043)	(0.063)	(0.045)
Gen. social trust	-0.010			
	(0.022)			
Trust in acquaintances		0.026**		
		(0.008)		
Trust in co-nationals			0.035*	
			(0.014)	
Trust in neighbors				-0.010
				(0.009)
Present economy	0.012***	0.000	-0.004	0.013***
	(0.003)	(0.003)	(0.006)	(0.003)
Relative deprivation	-0.001	0.000	0.007	-0.001
	(0.004)	(0.004)	(0.007)	(0.004)
Education	0.038***	0.039***	0.037***	0.037***
	(0.002)	(0.002)	(0.004)	(0.002)
Age	-0.003***	-0.003***	-0.003***	-0.002***
	(0.000)	(0.000)	(0.001)	(0.000)
Corruption: president	0.062***	0.061***	0.066***	0.063***
	(0.006)	(0.006)	(0.011)	(0.006)
Corruption: parliament	-0.001	0.003	-0.005	-0.001
	(0.006)	(0.006)	(0.012)	(0.006)
Corruption: police	0.002	0.002	-0.001	-0.001
	(0.005)	(0.005)	(0.009)	(0.005)
AIC	135382.494	144056.163	50702.343	137543.499
BIC	135497.915	144172.407	50804.376	137659.109
Log Likelihood	-67678.247	-72015.082	-25338.172	-68758.750
Observations	53,027	56,491	18,934	53,799
Number of countries	33	33	20	33

***$p < 0.001$; **$p < 0.01$; *$p < 0.05$

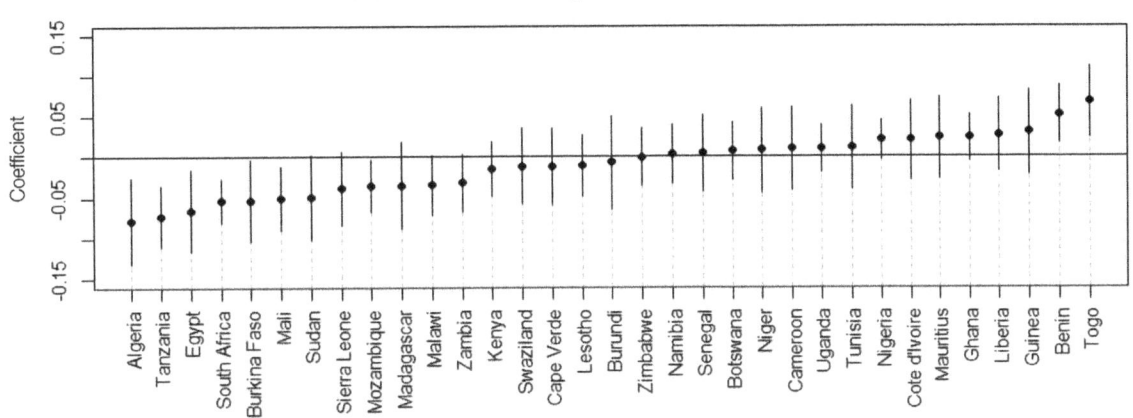

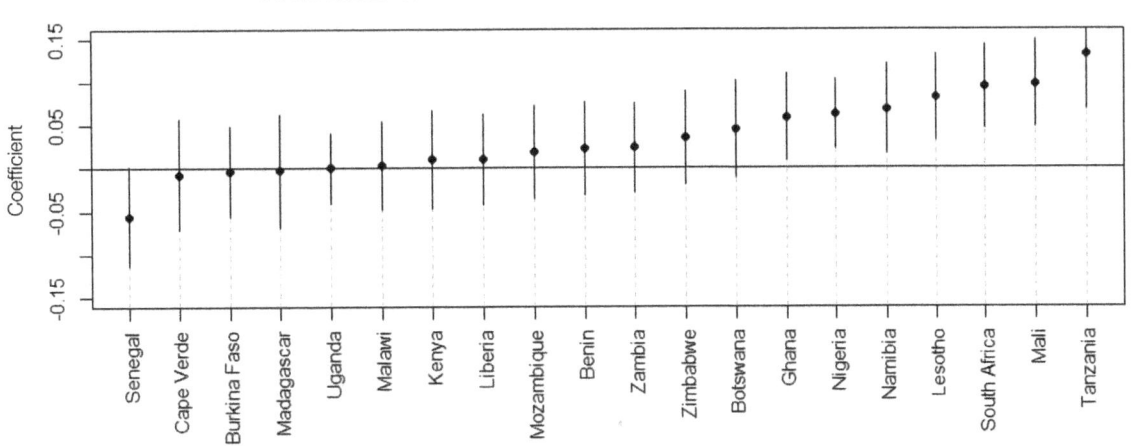

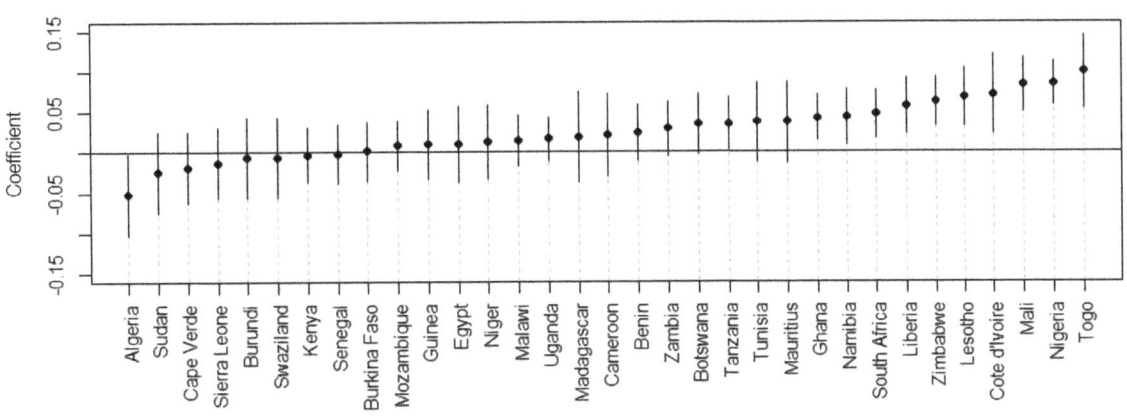

FIGURE 10. Comparison of Cross-Country Coefficients for Potential Mobilization

Figure 10 includes the unstandardized coefficients from the hierarchical model for each of the countries in the sample. I have included the three forms of trust that conformed to predictions. These demonstrate the country-by-country variation within different types of trust and also demonstrate how different forms of trust operate within a single country.

Statistical Information from Chapter 3

In Chapter 3, the monograph tests whether individual-level trust shapes justification for violent action, as well as whether aggregated forms of trust correspond with lower proportions of violent action in a given country. In this chapter, additional forms of trust were examined, including trust in diverse populations and trust in one's ethnic ingroup. Table 9. Descriptive Statistics of Ingroup and Outgroup Trust Variables displays the descriptive statistics for each of these variables.

Table 9. Descriptive Statistics of Ingroup and Outgroup Trust Variables

TYPE OF TRUST	MIN.	1ST QUART.	MEDIAN	MEAN	3RD QUART.	MAX
Trust in ingroup	0.00	1.00	2.00	1.68	3.00	3.00
Trust in diverse population	0.00	1.00	1.00	1.37	2.00	3.00

Table 10. Linear Regression on Justification of Violent Action

	MODEL 1	MODEL 2	MODEL 3	MODEL 4	MODEL 5
(Intercept)	2.027***	2.094***	2.020***	2.179***	2.153***
	(0.045)	(0.051)	(0.055)	(0.098)	(0.090)
Gen. social trust	-0.034***				
	(0.011)				
Trust in neighbors		-0.040***			
		(0.011)			
Trust in acquaintances			-0.029**		
			(0.012)		
Trust in same ethnic group				-0.049**	
				(0.020)	
Trust in diverse population					-0.045**
					(0.019)
Female	-0.028***	-0.026***	-0.026***	-0.019	-0.021
	(0.008)	(0.008)	(0.010)	(0.014)	(0.014)
Present economy	0.010***	0.010***	0.016***	-0.005	-0.007
	(0.004)	(0.004)	(0.004)	(0.006)	(0.006)
Relative deprivation	-0.001	0.000	0.004	-0.010	-0.007
	(0.004)	(0.004)	(0.005)	(0.008)	(0.008)
Education	-0.007***	-0.010***	-0.006**	-0.017***	-0.016***
	(0.002)	(0.002)	(0.003)	(0.004)	(0.004)
Age	-0.002***	-0.002***	-0.002***	-0.003***	-0.003***
	(0.000)	(0.000)	(0.000)	(0.001)	(0.001)
AIC	200690.716	203426.204	139382.293	59754.601	59242.155
BIC	200772.928	203526.839	139478.721	59842.021	59329.490
Log Likelihood	-100336.358	-101702.102	-69680.147	-29866.301	-29610.078
Num. obs.	68510	69472	47388	20895	20735
Num. groups: country_string	34	34	34	16	16

***$p < 0.01$; **$p < 0.05$; *$p < 0.1$

As with the hierarchical models in Chapter 2, this set of models also provides coefficients that can be analyzed at the country level. These are found in Figure 11. Comparison of Cross-Country Coefficients for Justification of Violent Action. One interesting observation is that, when measuring trust in neighbors and acquaintances, Algeria demonstrates the largest negative correlation with the justification of violent action. However, this correlation seems to be reverse in the earlier coefficients pertaining to potential mobilization in Figure 10. Comparison of Cross-Country Coefficients for Potential Mobilization

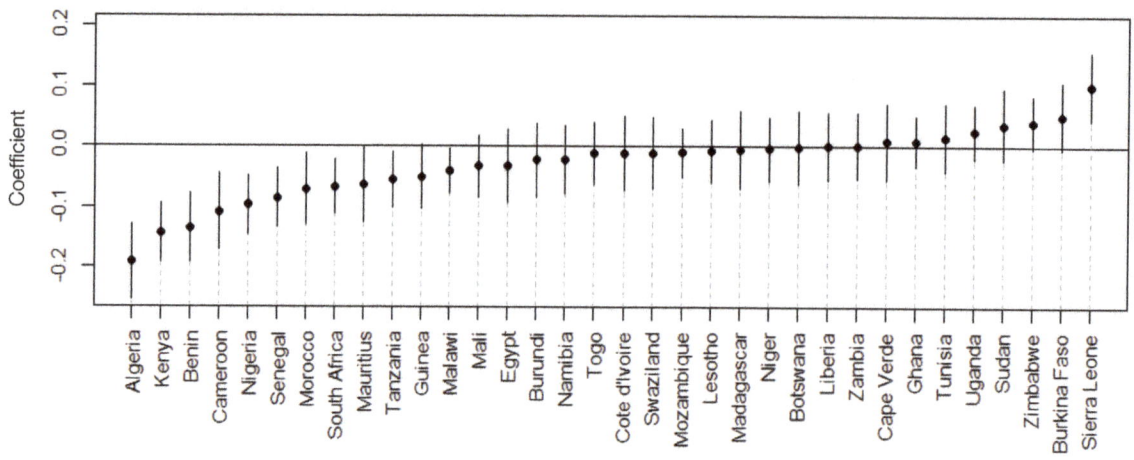
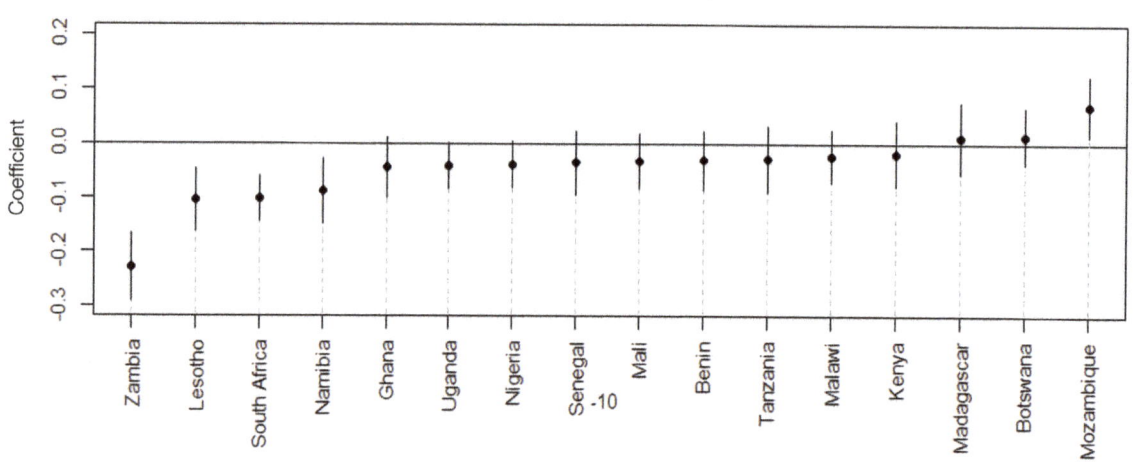
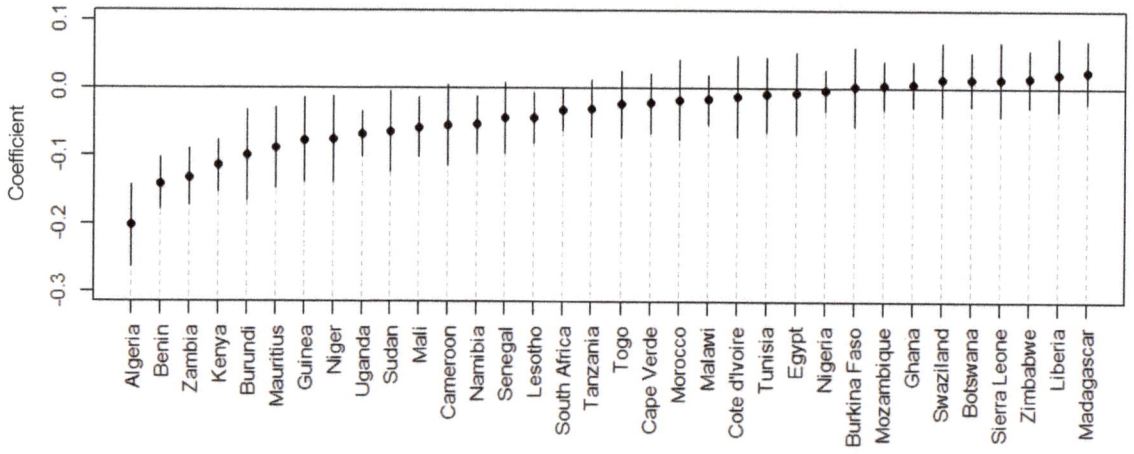

FIGURE 11. Comparison of Cross-Country Coefficients for Justification of Violent Action

Table 11. Linear Regression on Proportion of Conflict That is Violent presents the results of a hierarchical linear regression that regresses the proportion of total conflict that is violent on a series of trust variables and other relevant covariates. The model includes random intercepts structured at the country level.

Table 11. Linear Regression on Proportion of Conflict That Is Violent

	MODEL 1	MODEL 2	MODEL 3	MODEL 4	MODEL 5	MODEL 6
(Intercept)	0.177***	-0.053	-0.065	-0.309	0.040	0.101
	(0.033)	(0.098)	(0.097)	(0.190)	(0.194)	(0.101)
Gen. social trust	-0.009		-0.376*	-0.454**		
	(0.082)		(0.198)	(0.198)		
Trust in same ethnic group		0.135	0.164	0.234**		
		(0.115)	(0.115)	(0.115)		
Trust in diverse population		-0.056	-0.033	-0.032		
		(0.122)	(0.121)	(0.119)		
Trust in co-nationals					-0.025	
					(0.063)	
Trust in acquaintances						-0.022
						(0.030)
Present economy				0.014	-0.165**	-0.082**
				(0.073)	(0.065)	(0.039)
Living situation				0.061	0.302***	0.147***
				(0.072)	(0.074)	(0.044)
Employment				0.358***	-0.238*	-0.176**
				(0.131)	(0.138)	(0.082)
Handling corruption				-0.077	-0.051	-0.002
				(0.066)	(0.078)	(0.036)
AIC	261.811	80.622	80.476	91.027	170.348	379.612
BIC	279.762	96.777	99.863	123.339	198.391	416.146
Log Likelihood	-126.906	-35.311	-34.238	-35.514	-77.174	-181.806
Num. obs.	657	187	187	187	246	711
Num. groups: countryname	34	16	16	16	20	34

***p < 0.01; **p < 0.05; *p < 0.1

Note: Dependent variable is proportion of total conflict (protests and riots) that was violent. Thus, an inverse correlation supports the prediction that more trust correlates with lower levels of violent action.

Statistical Information for the Conclusion

One of the recommendations made for activists is to develop broad narratives that appeal to an array of groups throughout society. The monograph suggests recruiting from labor unions, which tend to be filled with many different types of people. In order to justify this suggestion, a cursory statistical regression was run to evaluate whether membership in a trade union is correlated with increased trust in diverse populations. Table 12. Union Membership and Trust in Diverse Populations displays a bivariate ordinary least squares regression that tests the correlation between membership in a trade union and trust in diverse populations. The regression is hierarchical and includes random slopes and intercepts structured at the country level. The results indicate that membership in a trade union is positively correlated with trust in diverse populations. This relationship is statistically significant at the 99.9 percent confidence level.

Table 12. Union Membership and Trust in Diverse Populations

	MODEL 1
Intercept	1.385***
	(0.074)
Member of a trade union	0.048***
	(0.012)
AIC	61,206
BIC	61,254
Log Likelihood	-30,597
Observations	22,357
Number of countries	16

***$p < 0.001$; **$p < 0.01$; *$p < 0.05$

Do Survey Respondents Believe That They Are Speaking to a Government Agent?

One potential challenge may be that survey respondents believe they are actually speaking to a member of the government, which, if true, would likely skew the survey results. More specifically, the presence of this belief might actually stymie reports of potential mobilization. This monograph looks at a specific question found in the Afrobarometer in order to examine this. The last question asked before each survey interview queries respondents about who they think sent the interviewer. This comes at the end in order to extract the most truthful answer. Despite the fact that the Afrobarometer survey enumerators explicitly state that they are a private research organization, a large percentage of respondents truly believe that they are agents of the government. It is likely that this highly conditions the responses within the Afrobarometer. In order to test whether this shapes reported potential mobilization, the study examines whether there is a relationship between respondent perceptions that the survey enumerator is in fact a government agent and reported potential mobilization. As one might expect, respondents that believe they are speaking to a government agent are more likely to state that they never have engaged in protest and never would. Across all countries surveyed in Africa and across each round of the survey, 51.6 percent of respondents who stated that they would never join a protest believed they were speaking to a government agent. On the other hand, 45.8 percent of respondents that stated that they often engage in protests believed that they were speaking to a government agent. Fortunately, a statistical analysis of this demonstrates that even when respondents believed that they were speaking to a government agent, they did not substantially or significantly underreport their potential mobilization.

About the Author

Jacob Lewis is an Assistant Professor of Global Politics in the School of Politics, Philosophy, and Public Affairs at Washington State University. His research centers on conflict processes and political psychology in the African context. He holds a Ph.D. from the University of Maryland and has worked extensively in the fields of international development and public policy.